ROYAL COURT

The Royal Court Theatre presents

HERO
by E.V. Crowe

HERO was first performed at The Royal Court Jerwood Theatre Upstairs, Sloane Square, on Friday 23rd November 2012.

HERO is part of the Royal Court's Jerwood New Playwrights programme, supported by the Jerwood Charitable Foundation.

HERO

by E.V. Crowe

Cast in order of appearance
Danny **Liam Garrigan**
Joe **Tim Steed**
Jamie **Daniel Mays**
Lisa **Susannah Wise**

Director **Jeremy Herrin**
Designer **Mike Britton**
Lighting Designer **Rick Fisher**
Sound Designer **Ian Dickinson for Autograph**
Casting Director **Amy Ball**
Assistant Director **Rosemary McKenna**
Production Managers **Emma Boyns & Tariq Rifaat**
Stage Managers **Bonnie Morris & Ralph Buchanan**
Stage Manager Work Placement **Stuart Campbell**
Costume Supervisor **Iona Kenrick**
Set built by **Richard Martin**

The Royal Court & Stage Management wish to thank the following for their help with this production: LYON Equipment Ltd, ORTLIEB, Leisure Sinks (part of the AGA Rangemaster Group), Binatone, ETT, CatEye Lights.

THE COMPANY

E.V. CROWE (Writer)

FOR THE ROYAL COURT: Kin, One Runs the Other Doesn't (Hung Over - Election Shorts Rough Cut).

OTHER THEATRE INCLUDES: Young Pretender (nabakov/Escalator East to Edinburgh/Hull Truck with Watford Palace/Mercury Theatre, Colchester); Live Feed/I'm Going to Show You (ROTOR/Siobhan Davies Studios); A Just Act (Clean Break); Charged: Doris Day (Clean Break/Soho).

E V Crowe was a member of the Royal Court Theatre Young Writers' Programme & Super Group, & has been on attachment to the Royal Court & National Theatres. She is currently under commission to the National, Watford Palace, & Unicorn Theatres.

MIKE BRITTON (Designer)

FOR THE ROYAL COURT: That Face, The Vertical Hour.

OTHER THEATRE INCLUDES: Abigail's Party (West End/Menier/Bath); Broken Glass (West End); The Taming of the Shrew, Much Ado About Nothing, A Midsummer Night's Dream, Antony & Cleopatra, Coriolanus (Globe); Rudolf (Vienna/Tokyo); Romeo & Juliet (Tokyo/Osaka); Tis Pity She's a Whore, Hay Fever, Dial M for Murder (West Yorkshire Playhouse); A Kind of Alaska, Krapp's Last Tape, Faith Healer (Bristol Old Vic); The Deep Blue Sea, Nijinsky (Chichester Festival); Statement of Regret (National); The Winter's Tale, Pericles, Madness in Valencia (RSC); The Promise, The Late Middle Classes (Donmar); Period of Adjustment (Almeida); Broken Glass, Walk Hard (Tricycle); Glass Eels, Comfort Me With Apples (Hampstead); The Tales Of Ballycumber, The Three Sisters (Abbey); Henry V, Mirandolina (Royal Exchange, Manchester); Wuthering Heights, The Lady From The Sea, She Stoops to Conquer (Birmingham Rep); Les Liaisons Dangereuses, Arsenic & Old Lace, People at Sea (Salisbury Playhouse).

IAN DICKINSON (Sound Designer)

FOR THE ROYAL COURT: The River, Haunted Child, Jerusalem (& West End/Broadway), Spur Of The Moment, Wig Out!, Now or Later, Gone Too Far!, Rhinoceros, My Child, The Seagull (& Broadway), Krapp's Last Tape, Drunk Enough To Say I Love You?, Piano/Forte, Rock 'n' Roll (& West End/Broadway), Motortown, The Eleventh Capital, Rainbow Kiss, The Winterling, Alice Trilogy, Fewer Emergencies, Way to Heaven, The Woman Before, Stoning Mary, Breathing Corpses, Wild East, Dumb Show, Shining City, Lucky Dog, Blest Be the Tie, Ladybird, Notes on Falling Leaves, Loyal Women, The Sugar Syndrome, Blood, Playing the Victim, Fallout, Flesh Wound, Hitchcock Blonde, Black Milk, Crazyblackmuthafuckin'self, Caryl Churchill Shorts, Push Up, Fucking Games, Herons.

OTHER THEATRE INCLUDES: This House, The Curious Incident Of The Dog In The Night-time, 13, Season's Greetings, After The Dance, Our Class, All's Well That Ends Well, Death & The King's Horseman, Harper Regan, The Hothouse, Pillars of the Community (National); Absent Friends (West End); A Midsummer Night's Dream (Regent's Park); Top Girls (Out of Joint/Trafalgar Studios/tour); Two Gentlemen Of Verona (Derngate); South Downs/The Browning Version (Chichester & West End); Children's Children, A Delicate Balance, Mrs Klein (Almeida); The Misanthrope (Comedy); Little Voice (Vaudeville); Othello, Much Ado About Nothing, Night of the Soul, The Whore's Dream (RSC).

RICK FISHER (Lighting Designer)

FOR THE ROYAL COURT: Tribes, On Insomnia & Midnight, A Number, Far Away (& NY Theatre Workshop), My Zinc Bed, Via Dolorosa (& Broadway), The Old Neighbourhood, Fair Game, Hysteria, The Changing Room, Rat in the Skull (Royal Court Classics), King Lear, Six Degrees of Separation (& Comedy), The Queen & I (& Vaudeville), Serious Money (& Wyndham's/Broadway), Bloody Poetry, Three Birds Alighting on a Field, A Mouthful of Birds.

OTHER THEATRE INCLUDES: 55 Days, Chariots of Fire (& Gielgud), The Judas Kiss (Hampstead); Richard III, Merchant of Venice (RSC); Billy Elliot the Musical (Victoria Palace); An Inspector Calls (West End).

DANCE INCLUDES: Matthew Bourne's Swan Lake.

OPERA INCLUDES: Seventeen operas for Santa Fe Opera; Tsarina's Slippers, Wozzeck (ROH); Turnadot (ENO).

AWARDS INCLUDE: Olivier Awards for Best Lighting Design (Hysteria, Machinal, Moonlight, Chips With Everything/Lady in the Dark); Tony Awards for Best Lighting Design (Billy Elliot the Musical, An Inspector Calls).

LIAM GARRIGAN (Danny)

THEATRE INCLUDES: Moonlight (Donmar); Otherwise Engaged (Criterion); The Anniversary (ACT/Mark Goucher/St. Elmo Productions); The Anniversary (Liverpool Playhouse/ACT); Honeymoon Suite (ETT).

TELEVISION INCLUDES: Strike Back, The Night Watch, Raw, Land Girls, Pillars of the Earth, Agatha Christie's Miss Marple: They Do It With Mirrors, Blue Murder, He Kills Coppers, The Chase, Silent Witness, Ultimate Force, Holby City.

JEREMY HERRIN (Director)

FOR THE ROYAL COURT: Haunted Child, The Heretic, Kin, Spur of the Moment, Off The Endz, The Priory, Tusk Tusk, The Vertical Hour, That Face (& Duke of York's).

OTHER THEATRE INCLUDES: This House, Statement of Regret (National); Absent Friends, Death & the Maiden (Harold Pinter); Uncle Vanya, South Downs (Chichester Festival); Much Ado About Nothing (Globe); Marble (Abbey, Dublin); The Family Reunion (Donmar); Blackbird (Market Theatre, Johannesburg); Sudden Collapses in Public Places, The Boy on the Swing, Gathered Dust & Dead Skin, The Lovers, Our Kind of Fun, Toast, Dirty Nets, Smack Family Robinson, Attachments, From the Underworld, The Last Post, Personal Belongings, ne1, Knives in Hens (Live).

TELEVISION INCLUDES: Dead Terry, Warmth, Cold Calling.

FILM INCLUDES: Linked.

Jeremy is an Associate Director of the Royal Court.

ROSEMARY MCKENNA (Assistant Director)

AS DIRECTOR, THEATRE INCLUDES: Anna in Between (Dublin Festival Fringe); Heroin(e) for Breakfast (Smock Alley); Bedbound (& Samuel Beckett), The Living End (New Theatre, Dublin); The Importance of Being Earnest (Samuel Beckett); Christmas Time (The Poly, Cornwall), The Pillowman, The Donahue Sisters (Players').

AS ASSISTANT DIRECTOR, THEATRE INCLUDES: Improbable Frequency (Gaiety); The Housekeeper (Project Arts Centre); Medea (Samuel Beckett).

Rosemary is currently a director on the Rough Magic SEEDS programme.

DANIEL MAYS (Jamie)

FOR THE ROYAL COURT: Scarborough, Motortown, The Winterling, Ladybird, Just a Bloke, The One with the Oven.

OTHER THEATRE INCLUDES: Moonlight (Donmar); M.A.D. (Bush).

TELEVISION INCLUDES: Mrs Biggs, Public Enemies, Treasure Island, Outcasts, Ashes to Ashes, Hustle,

The Street, Consuming Passion, Plus One, White Girl, Half Broken Things, Saddam's Tribe, Consent, Funland, Class of '76, Top Buzzer, Beneath the Skin, Keen Eddie, Bodily Harm, NCS, Dead Casual, In Deep, EastEnders.

FILM INCLUDES: Byzantium, Welcome to the Punch, Made in Dagenham, Nanny McPhee & the Big Bang, Tin Tin, The Firm, Red Riding 1975 & 1983, Mr Nobody, Hippie Hippie Shake, Shifty, The Bank Job, Atonement, Middletown, A Good Year, The Secret Life of Words, Vera Drake, Best Man, Rehab, All or Nothing, Pearl Harbour.

RADIO INCLUDES: Living with Mother, The Caretaker, Peter Pan in Scarlet.

AWARDS INCLUDE: Palmare Television Festival Award for Best Actor (Rehab).

TIM STEED (Joe)

FOR THE ROYAL COURT: The Pride.

OTHER THEATRE INCLUDES: Rocket to the Moon (National); Salome (Headlong); Volpone/The Duchess of Malfi (Greenwich); Much Ado About Nothing (Open Air); All My Sons (Liverpool Playhouse); Silverland (Arcola); Cigarettes & Chocolate & Hang Up (Kings' Head); Mere Mortals (Old Red Lion); 7 Blows (Pleasance); The Importance of Being Earnest (Theatre Royal, Northampton); Amoeba Project (Out of Joint); An Inspector Calls (Garrick); The Cows are Mad & Election Night at the Courtyard (BAC/The Red Room); Anne Frank (Festival Company); Threepenny Opera (City Centre, New York).

TELEVISION INCLUDES: A Young Doctor's Notebook, Holby City, The Town, Twenty Twelve, Garrow's Law, Casualty, The Bill, Peep Show, Diary of a Somebody, Rhona, Happy Birthday Shakespeare, Poirot, Blonde Bombshell.

FILM INCLUDES: Franklyn, Amongst Friends, Crush 472.

SUSANNAH WISE (Lisa)

FOR THE ROYAL COURT: Seven Jewish Children, Where Do We Live.

OTHER THEATRE INCLUDES: A Doll's House (Young Vic); The Holy Rosenbergs, Sanctuary, The Prime of Miss Jean Brodie (National); Soho Streets (Soho); Rabbit (Old Red Lion/Trafalgar Studios); Rabbit (Brits off Broadway); Festen (Lyric Hammersmith); The Unthinkable, Hay Fever (Sheffield Crucible); When Harry Met Sally…(Haymarket West End); Three Sisters (Playhouse West End); Life After George (Duchess West End); Three Sisters, Heartbreak House (Chichester Festival); The Dispute/The Critic, The Candidate (Royal Exchange, Manchester); Featuring Loretta (Hampstead).

OPERA INCLUDES: The Fairy Queen (Glyndebourne/The Proms).

TELEVISION INCLUDES: Derek, Le Grand, Freddi, Law & Order, U Be Dead, EastEnders, Peep Show, The Time of your Life, The Complete Guide to Parenting, Holby City, IT Crowd, Secret Smile, Soundproof, Vital Signs, Midsomer Murders, Kavanagh Q.C. Special, In a Land of Plenty, Staying Alive, The Tenant of Wildfell Hall, Eskimo Day, Faith in the Future, Casualty, Doctors, Bliss, The Strawberry Tree.

FILM INCLUDES: An Ideal Husband, Brittanic.

RADIO INCLUDES: Bar Mitzvah Boy.

JERWOOD CHARITABLE FOUNDATION

Jerwood New Playwrights is a longstanding partnership between the Jerwood Charitable Foundation and the Royal Court. Each year, Jerwood New Playwrights supports the production of three new works by emerging writers, all of whom are in the first 10 years of their career.

The Royal Court carefully identifies playwrights whose careers would benefit from the challenge and profile of being fully produced either in the Jerwood Downstairs or Jerwood Upstairs Theatres at the Royal Court.

The programme has produced a collection of challenging and outspoken works which explore a variety of new forms and voices and so far supporting the production of 73 new plays.

These plays include: Vivienne Franzmann's THE WITNESS, Anya Reiss' SPUR OF THE MOMENT and THE ACID TEST, Penelope Skinner's THE VILLAGE BIKE, Rachel De-lahay's THE WESTBRIDGE, Joe Penhall's SOME VOICES, Mark Ravenhill's SHOPPING AND FUCKING (co-production with Out of Joint), Ayub Khan Din's EAST IS EAST (co-production with Tamasha), Martin McDonagh's THE BEAUTY QUEEN OF LEENANE (co-production with Druid Theatre Company), Conor McPherson's THE WEIR, Nick Grosso's REAL CLASSY AFFAIR, Sarah Kane's 4.48 PSYCHOSIS, Gary Mitchell's THE FORCE OF CHANGE, David Eldridge's UNDER THE BLUE SKY, David Harrower's PRESENCE, Simon Stephens' HERONS, Roy Williams' CLUBLAND, Leo Butler's REDUNDANT, Michael Wynne's THE PEOPLE ARE FRIENDLY, David Greig's OUTLYING ISLANDS, Zinnie Harris' NIGHTINGALE AND CHASE, Grae Cleugh's FUCKING GAMES, Rona Munro's IRON, Richard Bean's UNDER THE WHALEBACK, Ché Walker's FLESH WOUND, Roy Williams' FALLOUT, Mick Mahoney's FOOD CHAIN, Ayub Khan Din's NOTES ON FALLING LEAVES, Leo Butler's LUCKY DOG, Simon Stephens' COUNTRY MUSIC, Laura Wade's BREATHING CORPSES, Debbie Tucker Green's STONING MARY, David Eldridge's INCOMPLETE AND RANDOM ACTS OF KINDNESS, Gregory Burke's ON TOUR, Stella Feehily's O GO MY MAN, Simon Stephens' MOTORTOWN, Simon Farquhar's RAINBOW KISS, April de Angelis, Stella Feehily, Tanika Gupta, Chloe Moss and Laura Wade's CATCH, Mike Bartlett's MY CHILD, Polly Stenham's THAT FACE, Alexi Kaye Campbell's THE PRIDE, Fiona Evans' SCARBOROUGH, Levi David Addai's OXFORD STREET, Bola Agbaje's GONE TOO FAR!, Alia Bano's SHADES, Polly Stenham's TUSK TUSK, Tim Crouch's THE AUTHOR, Bola Agbaje's OFF THE ENDZ and DC Moore's THE EMPIRE.

So far in 2012, Jerwood New Playwrights has supported Nick Payne's CONSTELLATIONS and Vivienne Franzmann's THE WITNESS.

The Jerwood Charitable Foundation is dedicated to imaginative and responsible revenue funding of the arts, supporting artists to develop and grow at important stages in their careers. They work with artists across art forms, from dance and theatre to literature, music and the visual arts. www.jerwoodcharitablefoundation.org.

THE ENGLISH STAGE COMPANY AT THE ROYAL COURT THEATRE

'For me the theatre is really a religion or way of life. You must decide what you feel the world is about and what you want to say about it, so that everything in the theatre you work in is saying the same thing ... A theatre must have a recognisable attitude. It will have one, whether you like it or not.'

George Devine, first artistic director of the English Stage Company: notes for an unwritten book.

photo: Stephen Cummiskey

As Britain's leading national company dedicated to new work, the Royal Court Theatre produces new plays of the highest quality, working with writers from all backgrounds, and addressing the problems and possibilities of our time.

"The Royal Court has been at the centre of British cultural life for the past 50 years, an engine room for new writing and constantly transforming the theatrical culture." Stephen Daldry

Since its foundation in 1956, the Royal Court has presented premieres by almost every leading contemporary British playwright, from John Osborne's Look Back in Anger to Caryl Churchill's A Number and Tom Stoppard's Rock 'n' Roll. Just some of the other writers to have chosen the Royal Court to premiere their work include Edward Albee, John Arden, Richard Bean, Samuel Beckett, Edward Bond, Leo Butler, Jez Butterworth, Martin Crimp, Ariel Dorfman, Stella Feehily, Christopher Hampton, David Hare, Eugène Ionesco, Ann Jellicoe, Terry Johnson, Sarah Kane, David Mamet, Martin McDonagh, Conor McPherson, Joe Penhall, Lucy Prebble, Mark Ravenhill, Simon Stephens, Wole Soyinka, Polly Stenham, David Storey, Debbie Tucker Green, Arnold Wesker and Roy Williams.

"It is risky to miss a production there." Financial Times

In addition to its full-scale productions, the Royal Court also facilitates international work at a grass roots level, developing exchanges which bring young writers to Britain and sending British writers, actors and directors to work with artists around the world. The research and play development arm of the Royal Court Theatre, The Studio, finds the most exciting and diverse range of new voices in the UK. The Studio runs play-writing groups including the Young Writers Programme, Critical Mass for black, Asian and minority ethnic writers and the biennial Young Writers Festival. For further information, go to www.royalcourttheatre.com/playwriting/the-studio.

"Yes, the Royal Court is on a roll. Yes, Dominic Cooke has just the genius and kick that this venue needs... It's fist-bitingly exciting." Independent

6 Dec 2012 – 19 Jan 2013

in the republic of happiness by Martin Crimp

A family Christmas is interrupted by the unexpected arrival of Uncle Bob.

Who is he? Why has he come? Why does his wife stay out in the car? And what is the meaning of his long and outrageous message?

All we can be sure of is that the world will never be the same again.

A violent satire, In the *Republic of Happiness* is a provocative roll-call of contemporary obsessions.

Royal Court Theatre Productions and Ambassador Theatre Group present
Royal Court at the Duke of York's. St Martin's Lane, WC2N 4BG

Until 5 Jan

constellations by Nick Payne

An explosive new play about free will and friendship with the
original the cast **Sally Hawkins** and **Rafe Spall**.

A Young Vic and Royal Court Theatre production
At the Young Vic Theatre, The Cut, SE1 8LZ

25 Jan – 23 Feb

feast

by **Yunior García Aguilera** (Cuba), **Rotimi Babatunde** (Nigeria),
Marcos Barbosa (Brazil), **Tanya Barfield** (US) and **Gbolahan Obisesan** (UK).
A vibrant exploration of the magnificent Yoruba culture.
Part of World Stages London. International Playwrights: A Genesis Foundation Project

020 7565 5000
www.royalcourttheatre.com

⊖ Sloane Square ⇌ Victoria ⎋ royalcourt ⦿ theroyalcourttheatre

ROYAL COURT SUPPORTERS

The Royal Court has significant and longstanding relationships with many organisations and individuals who provide vital support. It is this support that makes possible its unique playwriting and audience development programmes.

Coutts is the Principal Sponsor of the Royal Court. The Genesis Foundation supports the Royal Court's work with International Playwrights. Theatre Local is sponsored by Bloomberg. The Jerwood Charitable Foundation supports new plays by playwrights through the Jerwood New Playwrights series. The Andrew Lloyd Webber Foundation supports the Royal Court's Studio, which aims to seek out, nurture and support emerging playwrights. Over the past ten years the BBC has supported the Gerald Chapman Fund for directors.

The Harold Pinter Playwright's Award is given annually by his widow, Lady Antonia Fraser, to support a new commission at the Royal Court.

Principal Sponsor

Supported by
ARTS COUNCIL ENGLAND

INDIVIDUAL MEMBERS

GROUND-BREAKERS

Anonymous
Moira Andreae
Allen Appen & Jane Wiest
Mr & Mrs Simon Andrews
Nick Archdale
Charlotte Asprey
Jane Attias
Brian Balfour-Oatts
Elizabeth & Adam Bandeen
Ray Barrell
Dr Kate Best
Stan & Val Bond
Kristina Borsy & Nick Turdean
Neil & Sarah Brener
Mrs Deborah Brett
Mrs Joanna Buckhenham
Clive & Helena Butler
Sindy & Jonathan Caplan
Gavin & Lesley Casey
Sarah & Philippe Chappatte
Tim & Caroline Clark
Christine Collins
Carole & Neville Conrad
Anthony & Andrea Coombs
Clyde Cooper
Ian & Caroline Cormack
Mr & Mrs Cross
Andrew & Amanda Cryer
Alison Davies
Matthew Dean
Roger & Alison De Haan
Noel De Keyzer
Polly Devlin OBE
Glen Donovan
Denise & Randolph Dumas
Robyn Durie
Zeina Durra & Saadi Soudavar
Glenn & Phyllida Earle
The Edwin Fox Foundation
Mark & Sarah Evans
Margaret Exley CBE
Leonie Fallstrom

Celeste & Peter Fenichel
John Garfield
Beverley Gee
Mr & Mrs Georgiades
Nick & Julie Gould
Lord & Lady Grabiner
Richard & Marcia Grand
Don & Sue Guiney
Jill Hackel & Andrzej Zarzycki
Carol Hall
Jennifer & Stephen Harper
Sam & Caroline Haubold
Anoushka Healy
Madeleine Hodgkin
Mr & Mrs Gordon Holmes
Damien Hyland
The David Hyman Charitable Trust
Amanda Ibbetson
Nicholas Jones
David Kaskel & Christopher Teano
Vincent & Amanda Keaveny
Peter & Maria Kellner
Nicola Kerr
Philip & Joan Kingsley
Mr & Mrs Pawel Kisielewski
Sarah & David Kowitz
Rosemary Leith
Larry & Peggy Levy
Imelda Liddiard
Daisy & Richard Littler
Kathryn Ludlow
Dr Ekaterina Malievskaia & George Goldsmith
Christopher Marek Rencki
Andy McIver
Barbara Minto
Shafin & Angelie Moledina
Ann & Gavin Neath CBE
Murray North
Clive & Annie Norton
Georgia Oetker
Mr & Mrs Guy Patterson

William Plapinger & Cassie Murray
Andrea & Hilary Ponti
Lauren Prakke
Annie & Preben Prebensen
Julie Ritter
Mark & Tricia Robinson
Paul & Gill Robinson
Sir & Lady Ruddock
William & Hilary Russell
Julie & Bill Ryan
Sally & Anthony Salz
Bhags Sharma
The Michael & Melanie Sherwood Charitable Foundation
Tom Siebens & Mimi Parsons
Andy Simpkin
Anthony Simpson & Susan Boster
Paul & Rita Skinner
Mr & Mrs RAH Smart
Brian Smith
Mr Michael Spencer
Sue St Johns
The Ulrich Family
The Ury Trust
Amanda Vail
Constance Von Unruh
Ian & Victoria Watson
Matthew & Sian Westerman

BOUNDARY-BREAKERS

Anonymous
Katie Bradford
Piers & Melanie Gibson
David Harding
Steve Kingshott
Emma Marsh
Philippa Thorp
Mr & Mrs Nick Wheeler

MOVER-SHAKERS

Eric Abraham
Anonymous
Mr & Mrs Ayton MBE
Lloyd & Sarah Dorfman
Lydia & Manfred Gorvy
Mr & Mrs Roderick Jack
Duncan Matthews QC
Miles Morland
Ian & Carol Sellars
Edgar & Judith Wallner

MAJOR DONORS

Rob & Siri Cope
Cas Donald
Jack & Linda Keenan
Deborah & Stephen Marquardt
NoraLee & Jon Sedmak
Jan & Michael Topham
Stuart & Hilary Williams Charitable Foundation

Thank you to all our Friends, Stage-Takers and Ice-Breakers for their generous support.

Hero

E. V. Crowe's plays include *Kin* (Royal Court), *Young Pretender* (nabakov tour), *Live Feed/I'm Going to Show You* (ROTOR/Siobhan Davies Studios), *Charged: Doris Day* (Clean Break/Soho) and *A Just Act* (Clean Break).

E. V. CROWE

Hero

faber and faber

First published in 2012
by Faber and Faber Limited
74–77 Great Russell Street, London WC1B 3DA

Typeset by Country Setting, Kingsdown, Kent CT14 8ES
Printed in England by CPI Group (UK) Ltd, Croydon, CR0 4YY

A CIP record for this book
is available from the British Library

ISBN 978-0-571-30056-3

2 4 6 8 10 9 7 5 3 1

For my family and friends

Acknowledgements

This play was developed with the support of the National Theatre Studio and the Schauspiel Theater in Frankfurt. Warmest thanks to Purni Morell and Andreas Erdmann for developing the play. I would like to thank all the writers who read it aloud and commented at the Royal Court 'mega group': Alexi K. Campbell, Michael Wynne, Marcelo dos Santos, Molly Davies, Anya Reiss and Penelope Skinner. My gratitude to Patrick Welch, Johann Hari, Shaun Dellenty, Ruth Fitzsimons, Giles Smart and Erik Hovland. Thank you also to Dominic Cooke, Chris Campbell, Jeremy Herrin and everyone at the Royal Court.

Characters

Danny
thirties

Joe
thirties

Jamie
thirties

Lisa
thirties

In a rapidly developing part of town, by the river

DANNY'S SCENES
take place in Joe and Danny's big, modern, light kitchen

JAMIE'S SCENES
take place in Jamie and Lisa's smaller, darker kitchen

HERO

Act One: Danny

ONE

Danny and Joe's kitchen/living room.

Danny When the lady was here – Carolin.
She wanted me to talk about myself. Some stuff.
I told her –
I make different kinds of bread. I could see that when she looked at me, and I wasn't even wearing my death metal T-shirt, she questioned that I was familiar with yeast. That I was known to flour. Even though the room did smell of freshly baked bread, I could see she wasn't sure. And it wasn't even a ploy. It wasn't a tactic to get her to like me. We're not *selling* the flat . . . I'd forgotten to bake the bread for the school fair, and I had to do it there and then, or I'd be going round looking for rustic organic bakeries so that I could buy the bread that I said I would bake. I was perfectly willing to fake it, but it seemed easier to just bake – the bread. There was time to get it in the oven before she came. And Joe said, Joe said, it will smell homey. It will make our place smell like home.
First time she met me, what I didn't tell her, this is *before* the workshops, *before* going to panel, was why I moved down south in the first place. She didn't ask in fact. Not specifically. I didn't tell her that it is my personal opinion that proportionally more people who live in the north are twats when directly compared with a southern population. Call it south of Birmingham.

Joe comes in, listens.

There are significantly less twats south of 'the Birmingham divide'. There've been studies. I'll move back in ten years now I've said that.

I didn't tell her that when I was growing up in Sheffield I used to wear a yellow bomber jacket. Bright yellow, like I was going out fishing. And that my brother Alex loved that jacket. I mean he would go on and on and on at me for having it and telling me that he would swap whatever shite bag of clothes with skater logos he had for it and so on. I'd always say, 'No. And don't be a twat.'

It is my belief that every lad growing up somewhere gets shit now and again and it's usually from an older group of twats who want to kick your head in for no reason. I had a group of twats. There were five or six of them with fuck-all to do except follow me home and explain in detail how they were going to kick the shit out of me. I'd run for it, and I'm fast. Lucky for me, my twats were slow runners. Most twats in Sheffield are under-performers in sprint. (*To Joe.*) In the rack.

Joe goes again.

If they can sprint, really go fast, they're probably not a twat.

When I asked Mum, on a Friday night where my jacket was and she told me Alex had taken it, I could have killed him.

Joe comes back eating an apple.

I went up to his room to set an elaborate death trap and find something to borrow, because I was just about to leave the house to go out with the lads and it was fucking biblical outside. I took this bag-of-shite jacket off his floor, sort of tailored, and put it on because I didn't want to die of hypothermia and I had fuck-all else to wear.

That night, coming out the pub, someone whispered to me that they thought I looked beautiful. 'Beautiful'! This is fucking Friday night in Sheffield! I never forgot that. It must have been the jacket, it was sort of tailored in, and it gave me a line, I'd not had before. I looked good, I felt good, surprisingly. (*Joking.*) Alex was still going to die. I was going to kill him!

When they told Mum they'd found him dead. That the group of twats, my group of twats had chased him up the main street and he'd slipped and cracked his head on a bollard. I wanted to say to Mum that I felt sad and that now I would want to leave. Sheffield was full of twats and Sheffield had killed my brother. That I wanted the jacket back, to remember. I wanted to say stuff like that. But at no point, even when I was really fucking sad, did I think, that should have been me.

I know Mum thinks Alex would have got her grandkids faster. But like fuck he would. He couldn't even steal a jacket without getting killed, let alone go out, get married and bring her back knocked up.

None of that bollocks, if one of us was going to get lost, it was always going to be Alex. He'd say the same himself.

Sheffield's done now – past.

You can't tell that story anyway without saying 'twat'. She said the panel would look at all the information, assess it, make a decision.

Danny takes a dish out of the oven.

Joe Did they call?

Danny No.

Joe Did you check for messages?

Danny Yes.

Joe And?

Danny Nothing.

Joe Carolin didn't ring?

Danny No.

Joe It's too soon anyway. No one called?

Danny Oh. Jamie. He called.

Joe OK.

TWO

Danny is in the kitchen bit, Joe is in the sofa bit.

Joe I'm making a file.

Danny Are you?

Joe It's massive.

Danny 'Danny and Joe Adopt'. Let's see.

Joe You can see it when it's finished.

Danny Anything missing?

Joe I think you probably should have told Carolin about the nativity.

Danny Ha.

Joe I think you should have told her, so we'd have it on record.

Danny Ha.

Joe I think you should have told her . . .

The buzzer goes.

Danny Joe. Door.

Joe presses a button for the outside door, opens the inside door, Jamie comes right in the inside door, with a cycle helmet.

Joe Hi, Jamie.

They hug.

Jamie Was I supposed to wait at the main door?

He looks confused.

Joe I buzzed you in.

Jamie If it's already open am I supposed to buzz and walk straight in?

Joe Yeah.

Jamie looks at the door.

Jamie Hi, Danny.

They shake hands.

Cool workwear!

He points at Danny's high-top trainers.

Danny Nice one.

Joe Lisa away again?

Joe closes the door.

Jamie Yeah. God. She is.

Danny Have a seat, Jamie.

He gets up and opens the door again, brings in his bike and leans it against the window.

Jamie You can really see the whole of the city across the water. The whole this bit of it. And then you turn around and . . . we're in the countryside!

Joe It's a country-style kitchen.

Jamie That's exactly what I mean. It's very 'country'. And did you bake?! I can smell bread.

Danny For the fair.

Jamie It was nice. I got a loaf. Because . . .

Joe Because . . . Lisa's away.

Jamie She's going away. Yeah. It really reminds me of my grandmother's house in Devon. It's really very . . . They've got it just right.

Joe They're all like this, all the apartments.

Jamie Great. That's great. Everyone lives in the country together. It's like a village.

Joe They call these few blocks 'the village'. On the marketing.

Jamie Well, there you go!

Danny Was the bread OK?

Jamie I haven't had it yet. It's in my new *reflective*-trim pannier.

> *He points at the bike. The pannier looks full, and there are flowers coming out of the top.*
> *Silence.*

Joe (*to Danny*) Lisa goes away to rest.

Jamie She's tricky. She needs – a lot.

Joe (*to Jamie*) Can I tell him?

Jamie No, it's personal. She's on IVF.

Danny That must be stressful.

Jamie It's stressful. It's expensive. It's like a job. You have to just do the IVF. So she's gone to her mum's to rest and hopefully . . . it's very 'in the old days'. Women, having to rest and pray for a child to be 'bestowed upon them'.

Joe You should make a sacrifice. To the gods!

Jamie It does, it feels old-fashioned. It's like high-tech old-fashioned. (*Looking at the kitchen.*) Inner-city-country. Trendy-old-fashioned. Good-bad-good.

Joe I was just saying to Danny that he should have told our adoption lady, Carolin, about . . . first time we went to Willows Primary. And Danny was cold turkey. Two weeks, three weeks?

Danny Two weeks.

Joe Two weeks. We didn't have internet set up in the flat yet. Or a TV, and the DVDs were in storage. And it was like he went cold turkey. And . . .

Jamie I lent you a dongle.

Joe Yes! Cheers for that, mate . . . It was like he went cold turkey . . . and the whole world seemed new.

Danny Joe.

   Pause.

I couldn't even email . . .

Jamie 'LOL'.

Joe Two weeks, nothing! And so he goes to performance number one of the nativity play at Willows Primary and . . .
   He thinks it's *Hamlet*.

Danny I thought it was good . . .

Joe He called it 'art'. He cried.

Jamie And?

Joe So we *all* went.

Jamie And?

Joe Well it was *weird*. Almost European-weird.

Danny It was OK.

Joe Kids are shit actors. It wasn't even a bit magical. It was really really shit.

Jamie Didn't the dongle work?

Danny I was so hungry, for something . . . visual. Any entertainment. What a twat.

Joe He sold it to us hard! He was convinced. He convinced us!

Danny It was OK.

Joe (*to Jamie*) He does this. Puts his twist on things. Makes you go along with it blind.

Jamie He does. He absolutely does.

Danny notices.

Danny We had a nice evening.

Jamie I did the nativity that year. I organised it.

Silence.

Joe Did you? Oh Jamie. Sorry.

Danny Fucking hell, Joe. Did you, Jamie? Fucking hell, Jamie.

Jamie No! I'm joking. The nativity play's gay.

Pause.

They don't get me to do the nativity. I do the fete. I'm having a laugh.

Pause.

Though I don't think you should have told that lady that story.

Joe No. We didn't.

Jamie They want relevant, accurate information.

Joe We just think it's funny. We wanted her to know we're funny.

Jamie It is funny.

Pause.

Do you think they're going to get you a kid? I mean, are you on the list?

Danny We're waiting to hear back. Any day.

Jamie You could just steal one from school.

Danny Ha.

Jamie You could just kidnap one.

Danny Not that lot.

Jamie Yeah, cos they'll send you a good 'un. You'll definitely get the tough ones. The bad ones. You'll get a fuck-up kid.

Pause.

'LOL'.

Danny How's Lisa?

Joe Lisa's going away for a bit.

Jamie A little bit.

Joe Are you staying for dinner?

Jamie I just dropped in to talk to Danny actually.

Joe OK. I've got some work to do so . . .

Jamie Busy at the station?

Joe Tune in.

Jamie Media whore.

Joe Tweet me.

Jamie Fax me.

Pause.

Photocopy me.

Pause.

Hole-punch me.

Pause.

Joe Yeah!

Joe goes. Danny sits next to him.

Danny ?

Pause.

Jamie Oh. It's nothing really. I wanted your advice. Cool trainers, Danny.

Danny looks at his shoes, then back up.

Danny Shoot.

Jamie OK.

Danny I mean I'm listening.

Jamie I don't want you to do anything.

Danny No, I'll just listen.

Jamie You know Richard. Richard from work?

Danny is still listening.

Danny Sorry, yes.

Jamie What do you make of him?

Danny Me? I think he's a cock.

Jamie OK. OK, good. This is –

I heard Richard tell, Adam. I heard Richard tell Adam that I'm gay. He called me gay to Adam.

Danny When?

Jamie Today – the fete.

Danny What did Adam say?

Jamie Well, that's when they saw me.

Danny What did you do?

Jamie I told Richard I wanted to talk to him.

Joe comes back in to get his power lead. He looks at Danny.

Danny (*to Joe*) Richard.

Joe Tall Richard? He's a cock.

Danny Immature.

Jamie He's very immature.

Joe How old's he now?

Jamie Seven. Six, seven.

Joe Still, no excuse.

Danny and Joe laugh. Joe goes.

Jamie It's serious. It felt serious.

Danny Sorry, so what did you do after Richard, seven, told Adam, six, he thinks you're gay?

Jamie I asked to speak to him in the reading corner and I said to him. I said, 'What do you think being gay means?'

Danny Wow.

Jamie What?

Danny No, good. Where was his mum?

Jamie On the raffle.

Pause.

Danny You asked him that? Did he . . . he must have shat himself.

Jamie He thought about it. He really thought about it and then he said . . .

Danny What did he say?

Jamie He really thought about it.

Danny He won't have a clue.

Joe drifts back within earshot.

Jamie I didn't think he'd say anything. I thought I had nailed him on a technicality.

Danny What did Richard say?

Jamie Nothing.

Danny Must have said something.

Pause.

Jamie He said, 'It's when a man loves another man.'

Jamie watches Danny and Joe smile at each other across the room, pleased.

Danny Richard's all right. He's all right, Richard. His family are cocks. He's got an older brother. He's a proper little fucker. But Richard. He's OK.

Jamie Yes. I mean he's right. He said the right thing. The point is that he told Adam I'm gay. He's started a rumour.

Danny You're not gay.

Pause.

We've all met Lisa. We love Lisa. She made lovely stuff for the fete. I reckon don't worry about it.

Jamie Really?

Danny Let sleeping dogs lie.

Jamie I told him it was none of his business. And he'd never ever find out if I was gay or not. I made him feel really bad. His face went really red. He cried.

Danny OK.

Jamie I told him right up close so he wouldn't forget.

Pause.

I don't think he should be allowed to say stuff like that.

Danny The kids call everything gay. 'That sandwich is gay.' 'School is gay.' It's not nice.

Jamie It's not worth getting our knickers in twist about?

Danny No.

Jamie I told him off anyway.

Danny Sounds like it.

Jamie So you think I did the right thing?

Danny I think you did what felt right at the time and that's all we can ask of ourselves.

Danny pats Jamie's leg.

Jamie So you don't think I reacted wrongly?

Danny It's fucking hard to say.

Jamie But from your perspective?

Danny I don't know.

Jamie What do you feel?

Danny Like I said, Jamie, I think you did what you felt was right and right now that's good enough for me.

Jamie I'm a good teacher.

Danny Trust your instincts.

Silence.

Jamie I think I should have told him I'm not gay. Rather than taking the 'none-of-your-business' line.

Danny Maybe.

Pause.

Jamie Lisa's got this theory. She's into . . . stuff. That there's going to be a 'shift' soon. That suddenly, everything is going to – 'shift'.

Danny –

Jamie That it's written. In the stars. What *I* would more simply call cosmic data. If there's enough cosmic data to suggest it, then it happens, and you don't even notice until it's too late. The results can be pretty catastrophic. She calls it fate.

Pause.
A buzzer goes off next to the oven.

Danny Are you sure you don't want to eat with us?

Jamie I've got my bike. It's OK. And Lisa.

Danny ?

Jamie I'll have to call her otherwise. She'll need me to call her.

Danny See you Monday then.

Jamie Yeah. See you at school. (*Calling out.*) Joe, bye!

Danny and Jamie stand up. Jamie goes, with his bike.
    Joe creeps back in.

Joe He does have quite gay trousers on today.

Danny I was going to go for the shirt. But sure.

    They laugh.

We see a lot of those trousers.

Joe We live closer to them now.

Danny 'LOL'.

Joe He's a mate.

Danny He didn't come to the wedding.

    Joe thinks.

Joe He got mumps.

Danny I would have loved seeing his moves at the wedding on the dance floor. I can picture Jamie – shakin' it.
    Is he gay?

Joe No?

Danny Sure?

Joe Most gay straight man at college.

Danny Really?

Joe Loves Julie London. Has it on vinyl.

Danny I had a mate like that. Filthy ears.

Joe What?

Danny Mucky ears.

Joe Jamie's the same. Enough wax to lay the Yellow Brick Road.

Danny He's straight then.

Pause.

Joe He's a mate. An old college mate. I don't have many of those left.

Danny OK.

Joe He's a good . . . he's . . .

Danny He's OK.

Joe He's good.

Pause.

Danny Makes me want to get out the wedding photos. Look at all the nice people who did come, who we never see now.

Joe Danny.

Danny Mum . . . at our wedding . . .

Joe One guest we do see.

Pause.

Her one hundred and eighty?

Danny 'Son'? That?

Joe Her one hundred and eighty. Her big turnaround?

Danny She didn't change her mind, she showed it, that's all. You said it felt nice, to be approved of. You cried.

Joe Her one-hundred-and-eighty-degree wedding – 'You're my son now' – turnaround . . .

Danny Mum didn't have to change her mind.

Joe Kate's mum, after we broke up: 'I always knew he was a faggot.'

Danny Right.

Joe *She* changed her mind. And back again. Which means she never really changed her mind.

Danny I didn't know that.

Joe People don't change their minds about this stuff. It's too deep-rooted.

Silence.

Weddings though! They fucking work. You can lure them in. People like weddings. They just like them. People like hats. And ties. I like hats and ties.

Danny Our 'wedding-list toaster' does four pieces at once! For when two just isn't enough.

Joe They know how to respect it. People like things to be – neat.

Danny You like things to be neat.

Pause.

Joe I don't like those hair things, not-quite-a-hat-almost, just a thing stuck on your head – fascinators, though.

Danny No. Error!

Danny shrugs.

I don't think we need to worry. You can walk round naked in London and they'd respect it, no one would give a shit.

Joe You can't.

Danny You could walk round dressed as a . . . flamingo.

Joe You can't, that's a myth.

Danny You've never lived in Sheffield. Down here you can do anything you want.

Pause.

Joe Maybe.

Danny We'll tell our kid that.

Joe What?

Danny 'You can be who the fuck you like.' That can be our thing. The thing we say as encouragement.

Joe We don't know.

Danny Whatever the fucking consequences!

Joe OK.

Danny What?

Joe Nothing.

Danny What?

Joe We'll be normal parents.

Danny Like what?

Joe . . . Cautious.

Danny That's what I mean, yeah. And that's what I told the lady.

Joe Because we talked about this.

Danny I said what we said.

Joe I don't want us to look – naive.

Danny OK.

Joe Or . . .

Danny Or?

Joe Or political. They won't like it.

Danny I was myself.

Joe Yourself like we agreed?

Danny Yes, that one . . .

Pause.

Danny It's done now.

Joe We just have to hope for –

Danny What?

Joe Like we're sailors.

Danny We're –

Joe We have to hope for –

Danny We're *applicants*.

Joe – for fair winds.

Danny puts his hand on Joe's arm.

THREE

Danny finishes a can of beer, opens another. Joe is looking at a catalogue in a plastic cover.

Joe Makes me want to weep.

Danny They said you have to take it as it is.

Joe All their little faces.

Danny looks over his shoulder.

Danny That one looks a bit wonky.

Joe Danny!

Danny It's too sad otherwise.

Joe I know, but . . .

Danny 'Carmel', might grow up to be a psychopath, wonky.

Joe He's eleven.

Danny It's his destiny. It says.

Pause.

When do we get a current copy?

Joe looks at him.

Joe When we're through . . .

Danny All of these have been adopted by now.

Joe We hope.

Pause.

Danny Oh look, that one's got a moustache.

Joe It's a girl.

Danny Is it?! Can we please, can we have that one then?

Joe No, I'm not being outdone by our kid.

Pause.

I need a pretty one.

He flicks through the pages.

Danny Stop . . .

Joe I think we should get one that most resembles the kind of child we would have in the natural order of things.

Danny That's nice and everything. That's a bit . . . no, that's nice.

Pause.

'The natural order of things'? A bit . . .

Joe Fascist?! So?

Danny I'm comfortable with that.

Pause.

That one looks evil.

Joe Which one?

Danny That one.

Joe Yes he does. You can tell. We should call them and warn them.

Danny He looks all right. That one looks all right.

Joe What one?

Danny That one, with the hair.

Joe Funny face.

Danny Yes, him. I like his funny face.

Joe It's a bit lopsided.

Danny That's OK.

Joe You'd *choose* a kid with a lopsided face?

Danny Maybe.

Joe Why make our lives difficult? What if the other kids call him something rude?

Danny Like what?

Joe 'Lopsy'.

Pause.

Or 'Retard'.

Danny They won't.

Joe They might.

Danny No, he'll fit in. He'll charm them. He'll be cool.

Joe Not if he's got a lopsided face.

Danny It's not totally lopsided.

Joe They'll call him . . . 'asymmetrical'.

Danny At fuckin' *genius* school . . .

Joe They'll beat him up.

Danny Don't say that.

>*Joe shrugs.*

Tempts fate.

>*The buzzer goes.*

Who's that?

Joe Pizza.

Danny What if it's Jamie? I bet it's Jamie.

Joe No, I spoke to him earlier.

Danny It's family time. We're having family time . . . with the kids.

>*Danny pulls Joe back.*

Seriously.

Joe Door.

Danny We don't need to be sociable all the time.

Joe You're supposed to be the nice one.

Danny I am the nice one.

>*Danny presses the button for the outside door. Waits a beat, steps out, comes back in.*

I'll get my wallet.

>*Danny laughs, goes, pays for the pizza, brings in the pizza.*

Door goes again. Danny moves to open the outside door, then opens the inside door instead. Jamie's right there.

Danny Oh hi, Jamie.

Joe gets up, opens a can, joining in the drinking now.

Joe Hi, J. Don't you want to bring your bike in?

Jamie I walked.

Joe Oh, right? Didn't fancy the ride?

Jamie I was a bit. No. I didn't.

Danny Everything all right?

Jamie I didn't fancy the cycle.

Joe He can't cycle all the time I suppose. Makes it easier to 'pop' round though.

Jamie It's very easy either way. Danny . . .

Joe Makes it sort of effortless!

Jamie Danny . . .

Joe Do you want a beer, Jamie?

Danny Actually, Jamie, we were having some family time.

Jamie Family time?

Joe We're practising.

Jamie With *alcohol*? It's only Monday.

Joe The beer was Danny's idea.

Danny What's up, Jamie?

Jamie I shouldn't have come round. Sorry.

Danny It's not a problem.

Joe No problem. What's up?

Jamie Well.

Joe Is it Danny you're after?

Jamie No. I mean –

Joe Lisa, OK? You two have a fight?

Jamie Why do you say that? No. We haven't had a fight. Did she call you? She's away.

Joe No. I was joking.

Jamie She called Danny before.

Danny For a recipe.

Joe backs away, looks at Danny talking to Jamie like he's a child.

Jamie. What is it?

Jamie Is that pizza?

Danny Do you want some?

Jamie I thought you always cooked.

Danny Sometimes we get pizza.

Jamie What flavour?

Danny Hawaiian.

Jamie What?

Danny Hawaiian.

Jamie When I got home, I found these.

Danny OK. What is it?

Jamie In the letter box.

Danny Some flyers?

Jamie They say 'Faggot' on them.

Danny I can read.

Jamie Well, they've misspelt it, actually. It spells 'fagot'. Like a French word or something.

Danny I can read it, Jamie.

Jamie There were about fifty of them through the door. Fifty-two.

Danny Oh.

Jamie I was really shocked.

Danny I can see. I can understand. Joe, look at this.

Joe Horrible.

Danny It's horrible.

Jamie I felt really pretty shocked.

Danny Yes.

Jamie And someone knows where I live.

Danny You don't know for sure.

Jamie It's through my letter box.

Danny OK.

Jamie Someone thinks I'm gay and they want to scare me.

Danny It's bullying.

Joe It's bullying, I agree.

Danny But it's just bits of paper.

Jamie With 'faggot' written on them, or 'fagot'. Lots of pieces of paper. Lots and lots of pieces.

Joe You should call the police.

Jamie I did call the police.

Joe What did the police say about it?

Jamie Nothing they can do. If anything else happens, I tell them.

Joe OK.

Danny So they don't think . . . ?

Joe No . . .

Danny That's good then.

Jamie They don't think it's serious.

Pause.

I told them I had a hate crime done to me.

Danny Is it? Is this hate crime?

Jamie Yes, Danny. Of course.

Joe They didn't use scissors . . . just torn it.

Pause.

Jamie I told the police, I made sure they know I'm not actually gay. I told them I'm married to Lisa. And, anyway, they know it's sort of a case of mistaken identity.

Pause.

I wouldn't mind a beer now.

Joe Sure.

Joe gets him one, sits next to him with Danny. They both comfort him.

Jamie I haven't told Lisa. I don't want to worry her.

Danny I can understand.

Jamie I told the police about Richard.

Danny Richard?

Jamie I told them about Richard calling me gay and spreading rumours at the school.

Danny OK.

Pause.

Do you think Richard aged seven did this?

Jamie I don't know. Maybe his brother. His brother can't spell either.

Danny It's a jump to accuse Richard's family.

Jamie I didn't accuse. I just thought maybe. I thought it was relevant information. And his brother's got a record.

Danny For what, bad spelling?

Jamie Assault. Breaking and entering . . .

Joe I'd call that relevant.

Danny . . . colouring in over the lines?

Jamie The police said stuff like this happens quite a lot. But I feel really scared. I feel really shaken. That someone could hate me that much. For something I haven't even done, something I'm not.

Pause.

And even if I was. Still.

Danny It's bullying.

Joe It's terrifying.

Danny Don't say it's terrifying.

Joe Why not? I find it terrifying.

Danny Joe.

Joe Well, first this, then what? What's next?

Danny Nothing is 'next'. It's just a bunch of twats being twats.

Joe It never is just that.

Danny You can't stop people being twats. You just have to live your life. Get up, go to work. You just live your life.

Joe But they might come and get him.

Jamie It'll be those kids I've seen hanging about. You think they might come and get me?

Danny No. Joe! Stop it.

Joe These things happen, Danny.

Jamie Oh my God. Do you think they'll come back tonight?

Danny First it was a kid putting bits of paper through the door and now you've got him imagining a gang of gay-bashers.

Jamie Gay-bashers? What does that mean? Shit.

Joe People who bash gay people. It's a verb, I gay-bash, you gay-bash, we gay-bash . . .

Danny What I mean is, maybe they're not doing it because you're gay. Maybe they're doing it because you're . . . Maybe you've pissed off some neighbours. Or you were a dick to one of the kids on your street.

Jamie No.

Danny Or something else is going on.

Pause.

Maybe it's because you're you.

Jamie Thanks a bunch, Danny, you make them sound justified, or proportionate. If it's because I'm me, why did they call me a faggot?

Danny To be rude.

Jamie They think I'm gay.

Danny I'm just saying, it's conceivable that these people want to annoy you. They can annoy you by calling you gay, they don't want to annoy you because you are gay.

Jamie I've never had this kind of trouble before.

Danny No one's ever called you names? No one's ever wanted to kick your head in?

Jamie No.

Danny OK.

Jamie What?

Danny You can be a bit –

Jamie Like what?

Danny I've seen when we all go to the pub. A couple of times you've started something. I've seen you do it, you wind people up.

Jamie Mr actually-*is*-gay. Sorry, Joe, but . . .

Danny Yes, I am.

Jamie You are, I'm not.

Danny OK.

Jamie Joe! So don't you think it's weird?

Danny What?

Jamie Why am I getting the shit?

Danny What do you mean?

Joe What d'you mean?

Danny What?

Pause.

Joe (*to Danny*) He means it should be you. Don't you, Jamie?

Jamie No. And yes. Pineapple on pizza?

Danny Jamie? You think I should be getting the shit instead of you?

Jamie I'm saying. We both work at the school, we both work with kids, one of us is gay, the other is straight and I'm the one that is getting the shit. I'm just saying it's not fair.

Danny But life isn't fair, Jamie. It's hard enough actually being gay without going around volunteering to get other people's shit for them. You think I should volunteer?

Jamie So you do think it's because they think I'm gay rather than because I've wound someone up.

Danny I don't know, Jamie!

Jamie I haven't wound anyone up. They think I'm gay, Joe.

Danny I don't know, I think it's perfectly possible you've been a twat to someone who now hates your guts, I'd like to believe that takes precedence over you being gay or not. I'm not saying you deserve it either way. This is bollocks, either way. I just don't think it has anything to do with me. Sorry, Joe, but . . .

Jamie But they wrote 'faggot'. They're after me because I'm gay. Or they think I'm gay.

Danny What do you want me to do about it?

42

Jamie Nothing.

Joe The school knows he's gay. Everyone knows Danny's gay.

Pause.

Jamie Not everyone.

Joe The head teacher knows.

Jamie Not everyone.

Joe All the teachers know.

Silence.

Who?

Jamie –

Joe Who?

Jamie The kids don't know you're gay.

Danny Jamie.

Jamie This all started with Richard.

Danny Not really.

Jamie The kids don't know. None of them know you're gay.

Danny They don't know what gay is.

Jamie Richard does.

Danny You want me to 'come out' to my six-year-olds?

Jamie I'm just saying. Then everyone knows the truth.

Danny And I can be punished?

Jamie Punished? No!

Danny What then?

Jamie Then we're on an equal footing.

Danny If you're getting shit. It's not my fault. I don't know why these twats are after you, but I happen to think some people are just twats, and I don't take personal responsibility for other people's twattishness.

Jamie But you see it from my point of view?

Pause.

Danny I don't really.

Joe Jamie, I think you should probably try and go home now.

Jamie I was going to ask if you mind if I sleep here tonight. I feel, I feel scared to be at home on my own.

Danny Jamie.

Joe It's OK, Jamie.

Pause.

He can stay. I'll make up the other bed.

Jamie Pineapple and ham?

Danny Yes.

Jamie I'll try a bit.

Danny OK.

Jamie Do you mind?

Danny –

Jamie I'll take half. Do you have a knife?

He tears it ineptly, bites it.

(*Tasting it.*) Wrong! That's just wrong.

Joe I'll show you the other room.

44

Danny That's our kid's room.

Pause.
   Joe takes Jamie out.
   Danny sits eating the pizza.
   Joe comes back in.

Joe OK. Well.

Danny Fuck.

Joe He's always been like that.

Danny A twat?

Joe He's OK. A bit 'other', a bit 'Famous Five before the re-edit'.

Pause.

And he's having a hard time.

Danny But the way of him. The force of him.

Joe He was the same at college.

Danny That's OK then.

Joe Hang on, hang on, I'm on your side! There's no way you're going around telling all your kids you're lord of the dance.

Danny –

Joe No way, no fucking way.

Danny I'm not surprised people are after him.

Joe I feel really bad for him. He's a mate.

Danny He's a –

Joe But I definitely don't think we should do anything to rock the boat. Not until we hear back.

Danny I won't do anything.

Joe OK, good, because . . .

Danny Yes.

Joe Our application.

Danny Yes.

Joe *Yes.*

Danny I'm not going to do anything weird. And definitely not because Jamie's got a bee in his fucking bonnet.

Joe Jamie's anxious. About Lisa. Everything else. Lisa's a real job for him. A proper strain.

Danny *He's* anxious.

Joe We're doing what we're doing. We can only do this, if we go by the book. Announcing you're gay to minors is not in the book. That's in the other book.

If you do that, you're asking for it.

Danny Except that there's a criterion and we know we meet it.

Joe Yeah.

Danny So we don't need to worry too much about rocking the boat.

Pause.

Joe Don't tempt the adoption gods.

Danny Me being a primary teacher must help.

Joe They might not see it like that.

Danny Why?

Joe Mathematically speaking, I think the square root of male homosexual primary school teacher times one is paedophile.

Pause.

I love you.

Danny Jamie's a twat.

Joe He's OK.

Danny I have to work with him.

Joe Don't stress.

Danny Me? I don't stress.

Joe I forgot, you don't stress.

Danny You and me can't fall out.

Joe We haven't.

Danny No, I know.

Joe Just don't rock the boat.

Danny I haven't done anything wrong.

FOUR

Joe is sitting listening to Danny.

Danny And maths. Adding up, has to be about . . .
Queen Elizabeth, Assembly has to be about Queen
Elizabeth, literacy has to be about fuckin' . . . Queen
Elizabeth.
    That's how they do it now, they tie everything in to
one thing. Which is actually, philosophically, quite
interesting. So I'm thinking how the fuck can I tie sexuality,
or not sexuality, inclusion really, 'this', into the fucking
Elizabethan period.

Joe Danny.

Danny Hang on . . .

We've just finished this proper full-on drawing and painting session on the Spanish Armada, the Spanish fleet of boats sent out to attack the English coast and Sir Francis Drake, who sort of got lucky with all his little boats and managed to burn out most of the Spanish, the Spanish fleet. There are crayons and rubbers and pencils all over the place.

Half the kids have drawn these boats upended, sinking into the water, with sailors drowning or clinging on the edges, so I think – magic. We put these up on the walls.

After we look at all the pictures and I say confirming and supportive things about each of them, even the ones that look like blobs and lines, I get all the kids to help me turn over one of the tables so that it is sort of like a raft.

Danny re-enacts, doing all the voices.

Then I get the kids to imagine there is a storm coming, a great storm, and that they are within the Spanish fleet and they are drowning. So they have to wave their arms around and Ginny, this little Ginny, she goes for it, really pretending to choke and drown. And I'm on the raft, and I pretend to be the captain of the lifeboat and I get this other kid Nathan to be the first mate. So I call out, 'Who's that?' to Ginny, and she says, 'Ginny.' And I say, 'Ginny, what's you're favourite colour?' and she says, 'Blue.' And I say to Nathan, first mate, 'Do we let people whose favourite colour is blue on the rescue boat?' And Nathan's all confused, so I have to reassure him, it's OK. And he says, 'Yes,' so I re-affirm and say we let people who like 'blue' on the rescue boat, and we go through the process of 'rescuing' Ginny, and she's still in the zone, pretending to be cold from the cold water. Fuckin' fantastic. Gradually we rescue all the other kids and they all like different colours, some don't have a favourite colour, the cool ones don't, but we let them on the boat anyway. And then one kid says, 'You've let everyone on the rescue boat.' And I say, 'Yes, yes because we are a community here and we want to include everyone even if they are different to us.' And the kids seem happy with that. And no one wants anyone to drown. Though Ginny later 'dies' on the boat, sort of for fun. And everyone seems proud of our school and our community and our rescue-table-boat-thing.

And then Lilly wants to play the game 'again, again'. And I think OK, why not.

This time I'm out in the water as well and Ginny is the new captain, but I help her think what to ask. I get her to ask, 'Who do you live with?' So she sees Daniel drowning and says, 'Who do you live with?' and he says, 'My mum and dad,' and I say, 'Do we want to rescue Daniel who lives with his mum and dad?' and Ginny plays along nicely and says 'YES!' so Daniel gets on the table-boat-raft-thing. And I'm still doing the water noises, wind noises, and the occasional mast falling into the water. And encouraging everyone to wave their arms and shout for Ginny to help them.

So we go through a few more drowning kids, one lives with just their mum, another lives in a care home, and I wonder if it's right I made him disclose this, then it comes to me and I say I live with Joe my husband. And they don't say anything, I mean it doesn't go silent, they just absorb the information and pull me on to the boat.

Joe Danny.

Danny waits.

Danny And Joe, Joe, it was the most affirming fucking moment of my life.

Silence.

This is the next fucking generation and you know how they feel about homosexuality?

49

Pause.

I'm their teacher. I'm Mr Thompson and Mr Thompson
is married to another man. Mr Thompson is gay, but they
want me in their raft, in their community, they don't even
have to think about it. It was a weight lifted off my shoulders.
It was the most incredible thing I've ever experienced.
And that's when I knew, that the future is on our side.
We're going to get ourselves a kid to love and bring up.
And you know why? Because the next generation say fuck
it, it's fine. Mr Thompson and the like of him are all right
by us. And we're only six, we're the vulnerable and we're
all good with the gay. Some of us might be gay. But Mr
Thompson was straight with us, I mean honest with us!
    We're going to get that phone call today. I know we
are, Joe, I've got no doubt. This city is on our side. I've
heard it from its children. The children are on our side.

Joe 'The children are on our side'?

Danny Well, like, the future. You know what I mean.
We're lucky, we're in a time, we're on the cusp of things –

Joe We talked about you not saying anything while we
do our application.

Danny Sorry, but . . .

Pause.

Joe Is this Jamie?

Danny No, this really isn't about Jamie. I mean, yes, he
started it, but really he was right. Not about getting the
shit instead of him, but that the only people we lie to, we
deceive any more are the children, and there's no reason
to. Richard who is seven thinks gay is bad because he
doesn't know anyone openly gay, he doesn't know that
what he's saying has repercussions. I have a responsibility
to set an example, to be a responsible gay figure in their

lives. And also I don't give a fuck. I don't like being intimidated by an invisible force.

Joe I don't think parents are an invisible force.

Danny Who mentioned parents?

Joe Me, I'm thinking, me, as a parent.

Danny I thought this was about the application, not rocking the boat.

Joe It is.

Danny So why are you talking to me like we're at a parent-teacher meeting?

Joe I'm not.

Danny Feels like you've got a notepad and a custard cream.

Joe I can't say one hundred per cent . . .

Danny Go on.

Joe I can't say one hundred per cent about things like this, now we're having kids of our own.

Danny What?

Joe That I would necessarily want that my, our child, to be taught by someone . . .

Danny Someone what?

Joe Someone openly gay.

Danny Someone gay?

Joe Openly. It's something I've been thinking about.

Danny We've talked about this before.

Joe I know.

Danny You don't have a problem with it. You can't have a problem with it, actually.

Joe Well, most schools don't allow it, so it's a non-issue.

Danny But *in theory*.

Joe We aren't in theory.

Danny I don't know what you mean.

Joe You don't have to do a presentation is what I mean.

Danny Oh.

Joe I don't know. I don't know. It's not how I was brought up. And it never came up with me and Kate, or –

Danny Everyone at your work knows you're gay.

Joe Different.

Danny How is it different?

Joe I don't work with kids.

Danny Oh. I don't know what to say. I think I'm not getting you right.

Joe Primary school?!

Danny I think it's fine.

Joe Really? Do you really think that, or are you being over the top?

Danny I don't know.

Joe You do go over the top.

Danny I don't think I do.

Joe You get excited.

Danny Yes.

Joe It would make you feel better to be honest with the kids?

Danny Yes.

Joe It's not about you. Secondary school – yes, definitely. Primary school, not so sure.

Danny –

Joe It's not what they need to be thinking about.

Danny It's how the world is.

Joe They don't learn about *electricity* until they're fifteen. They just learn how to turn a light on. You can overload kids with . . . detail. I would be confused if I was them.

Danny Yeah.

Pause.

Are they giving you a reference, your work, for the adoption?

Joe Simon is, yes.

Danny You must feel very supported.

Joe That's not the same thing. And your work do support you.

Danny Hello?! Joe? Knock, knock.

Joe Look, you disregarded what we agreed.

Danny Yes, but . . .

Joe We *agreed*.

Danny Fucking hell.

Joe You can't just push for what you want.

Danny Why not?

Joe This is our agreement. We're only talking about the politics of it because adoption is political. In an ideal world, I wouldn't give toss. In the real world, things shape up differently. And I can't have children except by playing by certain rules. These are the rules – act normal.

Danny We are normal.

Pause.

I think you're nervous.

Joe Nervous?

Danny You feel nervous about being a dad, so you're putting that fear on to me.

Joe Fear?

Danny Soon as we get the phone call, Joe . . .

Joe I'm being – pragmatic. Act normal.

Danny Soon as we get the phone call, Joe. You'll realise I was right. That we are OK. That we can do what we like. We don't actually have to tiptoe around. We are approved of. No one thinks we're paedos. We don't have to make ourselves look like anything we're not. We're fine. We're approvable. You'll be an incredible father. I know you will. I just know it inside, I don't need their approval like you need it.

Joe I don't think she will call us. I don't think they will say yes at this rate.

Danny We're going to be parents.

Joe If we're lucky.

Danny No! Assume I'm knocked up. It's coming, ready or not, it's coming.

Joe She won't call, Danny.

Danny Ring-ring, ring-ring!

Joe They won't.

Danny Ring-ring, ring-ring!

Joe All I know is, when listeners ring up the radio station on every show, every day, thousands and thousands of Londoners, they're not saying nice things about people like us.

The door opens, neither of them notice. Jamie walks in covered in blood.

Danny You don't take those calls any more. That's ten years ago. You have no idea what people are saying now.

They notice him.

Fuck me. Joe, get a cloth or something. What the fuck happened. Did you fall off your bike?

Jamie No.

Danny What happened?

Jamie Nothing.

Danny and Joe stare at him a moment, just looking at him.

Danny Did someone do this to you?

Jamie Some kids . . . I got beaten up.

Danny How?

Jamie I don't know.

Danny Joe.

Joe What happened, Jamie?

Jamie On that bit of road between yours and mine. I just lay on the ground and they kicked me and I was there crying.

Joe It's OK, Jamie, it's not your fault.

Jamie I know it's not. I know it's not. I told you both, didn't I tell you this would happen?

Danny How did you get away?

Jamie What?

Joe It's OK.

Danny goes outside.

Jamie I didn't. I shouted, 'Look, I'm married.' But they didn't listen. It's not what they wanted to hear. I should have fought back. Danny would have fought back. Of course it's not my fucking fault.

Joe Danny can run fast.

Jamie No, Danny would have fought back. Fucking hell.

Joe It's OK, Jamie. Your eye's puffy.

Jamie Is it?

Joe Have you tried retracing your steps?

Jamie I didn't lose my wallet! (*He pats his pockets.*) Fuck, I did lose my wallet.

Joe Sorry.

Jamie I've seen them before, I think.

Joe You're here now.

Jamie It got worse today, right after Danny's . . .

Joe What?

Jamie His class.

Joe What did?

Jamie All of it. Worse and worse and worse and worse. For *me*.

Pause.

There was a shift.

Joe OK.

Jamie At the school and . . . then further out to round here.

Joe Really?

Jamie I could feel it shift.

Joe *I* told Danny not to.

Jamie It's made things worse.

Joe *You* told him to do it, Jamie.

Jamie But now I don't want him to have just gone and done it.

Joe He's not . . .

Jamie He's made a shift.

Joe . . . Danny doesn't have cosmic powers, Jamie.

Jamie My face says apparently he does.

Joe The thing with Danny . . .

Jamie Yes, he's . . .

Joe With Danny. Everyone loves Danny. People don't beat Danny up, they don't give him shit, because he already doesn't care. He's a bit untouchable. There's quite a lot of blood . . .

Jamie These lads would have a go. Definitely.

Joe OK.

Jamie Danny's a liability.

Joe It's OK, Jamie. I know Danny.

Jamie I'm sorry, Joe. I'm so sorry.

Joe It's OK.

Jamie No, I mean I'm sorry.

Joe What?

Jamie I'm sorry, Joe.

Joe It's OK. Shut up, will you?

Jamie I can feel the swelling now.

> *Pause.*

When we first became friends, then you were married to Kate, it was much easier, don't you think it was – nicer?

> *Danny comes back in.*

Danny Where are they now then, Jamie? These lads?

Joe What? Why?

Jamie I don't know. I'm trying to remember . . . They asked me who my boyfriend is . . . Who my little boyfriend is . . . They were going to really hurt me. So I think I told them Danny, just to get them to stop kicking me. So . . .

Joe What?

Jamie I'm up and down that road, aren't I? They must have assumed we're going out anyway. I don't know. Then I ran off –

> *He gestures far away.*

But I'm not very fast. Am I, Joe?

Danny You told them where we live.

Jamie Did I?

Danny You 'ran off' here?

Jamie That's right.

Danny You brought them here?

Jamie Brought? No!

Joe gets up.

Joe Danny! Let's go.

Joe studies Jamie a moment, unsure if he's telling the truth.

Danny Phone call.

Joe They'll have followed him.

Danny There's no one outside.

Jamie It's that bit of road. You can see right down it from yours to mine. Nothing to do, except eat fried chicken. They'll know I'm here.

Danny Take the car.

Danny Two minutes. Call the police on your way. Get them to meet you at Jamie's.

Joe What about you?

Danny (*quietly to Joe*) They won't come here.

Jamie hears.

Jamie Maybe better safe than sorry.

Joe Leave it, Jamie.

Jamie I want to tell him what I said.

Danny They're not going to come round here. Even if they do, they can fuck off.

Joe Danny, look what they did to Jamie's face. How many were there, Jamie?

Jamie Three, four. Four.

Joe Four of them, Danny. How are you going to fight off four people all on your own?

Danny Do what you like. You've probably got a residents' meeting or something to go to. I'll come over as soon as we get the phone call. I'm sorry, but I've got to take this call. It's important, then I'll come right round. Or you can stay here.

Jamie And I'm worried about Lisa. I haven't told her, I never went inside. I just came straight here.

Danny Then you better get back. Joe, take your mate home.

Jamie I'm sorry, Danny, I wasn't thinking. Maybe I run faster than I think. Maybe they don't have a clue where you live.

Pause.

Danny Why didn't you just say, 'Joe and Danny are gay, go and get them'?

Jamie nods, recognising the sentiment.

Jamie I wanted to show I'm on your side. That I like you, even though you're gay. Without not telling them the truth.

Danny Well, thanks very much, Jamie.

Jamie It felt like the right thing to do.

Jamie goes quiet.

Joe Jamie?

Jamie Sometimes I wonder what it would have been like for people like my dad. He came home at the end of the day and went like this –

Jamie sits, leaning back, hands behind his head, feet outstretched.

– and he just knew.

Danny (*to Joe*) Is he . . . concussed?

Jamie No announcement. No struggle. Head of the family. Kids. No pineapple. A very fine 'tash'.

Jamie runs his fingers along just above his top lip, tracing the stubble.

Called my mum 'baby'.
End of the working day – 'Hey, baby.' Then, like this –

Leans back again.

It's a tragedy.

Joe and Danny watch him, silent.

Danny No one's coming round. You'll see.

Jamie They were pissed. Like it was hilarious. Like they were on a day trip. I didn't know where else to go.

Joe Danny, I'm serious, let's go.

Danny I'm not twatting off down the road cos some twats are causing a fuss and missing our phonecall. Fuck 'em.

Joe Is this the city being on our side? It doesn't feel like it?

Danny I won't deviate course because of twats and that's it. Fuck off the pair of you if you like.

Joe Danny.

Danny It's OK. Go.

Joe I can't just go.

Danny Take Jamie.

Joe You'll be angry later.

Jamie Danny, will you just . . .

He puts Danny's hand in his.

For a moment.

Danny lets his hand go.

Danny Nothing's going to happen. I'm telling you –

Joe –

Danny You take Jamie, I'll take the call.

Joe You don't even know it'll be today.

Danny I do know. Cos of the kids and the moment I had today. And cos of the boat and all of that which you obviously think is bollocks. But I know a sign when I see one. It's a great big fucking sign, saying 'We're all right, do not be afraid, we're entitled to have a family, we'll be fucking good parents, as good as anyone else, and even a child knows that.' We know this because the children as good as said it, they've given us their blessing – the future says 'yes'. I'm not running out of my own home because some twats hump Jamie. Jamie, I'm sorry you got some shit, go home, see Lisa, talk to the police, then go to the hospital for your head. For the injuries to your head.

Joe, Jamie, I'm waiting for the phone call.

Joe It's after six o clock.

Danny Well, Joe, sometimes, people work late.

Jamie Danny . . .

Danny Jamie, fuck off.

Joe This isn't normal.

Danny Fuck you!

Silence.

Joe and Jamie leave. Danny acts relaxed, then locks the door behind them.

Danny waits. He gets out some flour and starts baking some bread.

After a while he hears banging on the outer door. He puts on an apron, continues.

They shove through the outer door.

A man starts banging on Danny's door.

Danny looks at the phone.

He carries on kneading the dough. The banging and shouting continues.

A brick knocks steadily against the glass top half of the door until it breaks through.

Danny continues.

Wait right there a moment!

The phone rings.

He picks up.

The banging increases. The door judders. Danny holds his hand, up signalling the noise should stop. It does.

Yes, this is Danny Thompson. Oh, hi. How are you? I'm fine I'm fine I'm good . . . Thanks for calling. We've been hoping you'd call today . . .

The noise starts.

One moment please, Carolin.

Danny walks over to the door, unlocks it and opens it.

Act Two: Jamie

ONE

A year ago. Jamie and Lisa's smaller, darker kitchen.
Jamie sits on a chair half dressed. He doesn't move for a bit.
Lisa comes in, sees him sitting there.

Lisa You'll miss it if you don't leave now.

She goes.
After a while she comes back.

Jamie . . .

Jamie What does it mean then if I don't go?

Lisa Karma-wise?

Pause.

Jamie Forget it.

Lisa I'm sorry, I thought that's what you meant.

Jamie What I mean is, I won't know how to act when I get there.

Lisa It's a wedding.

Jamie does the inverted-commas sign with his hands.

You'll be a guest. A friend.

Jamie I feel quite stressed at the idea of that. The where-to-put-myself-ness of that. A bit wobbly! You know.

Lisa You look a bit worn out now.

Jamie Do I? It's v. debilitating, isn't it? Working out . . . what is best.

64

Lisa Uh-huh.

Jamie I mean, I was . . . Kate was a mate.

Pause.

Jamie And Danny . . .

Lisa ?

Jamie They're moving up the road you know. Ten minutes. One of the new ones. Before it's built. They've bought it before it's gone up.

Lisa How long will that take?

Jamie Christmas.

Lisa Optimistic!

Jamie V. optimistic.

Lisa No!

Jamie Do they want to be us or what?!

Lisa Looks like they want to be us!

Pause.

Jamie Danny . . . he's nice! He's . . . It's like I'm six, he's the cool kid, you know? Danny's the cool one.

Lisa I think you're cool.

Jamie Last time I saw Joe, Danny was wearing young person trainers. High-tops.

Lisa You like those shoes!

Jamie I'd never put them on my feet. No one wears them.

Lisa You should!

Jamie He's the cool kid. Too cool for school. Like he's a celebrity.

Lisa What if he wears high-top trainers actually to school when he starts working at Willows next year?!

Jamie You can't wear canvas in January. 'LOL'. If he does then I'll leave. Just . . . sell up. Move to Spain.

Lisa Lovely!

Jamie Lovely oranges. Oranges squeezed, oranges with yoghurt for breakfast, duck alla oranges. Orange juice. People wearing espadrilles. No high-tops.

Lisa Sunshine in a fruit, oranges.

Jamie Joe wants me to show Danny around a bit.

Lisa You should.

Jamie They should have invited you as well.

Lisa I don't mind. It's a numbers thing, isn't it, they couldn't.

Pause.

Jamie (*remembering a further logic*) I've got the nativity to start conceptualising . . . there's a lot on.

Lisa You got stressed at our wedding.

Jamie Did I?

Lisa No!

Pause.

A bit.

Jamie Don't be silly.

Lisa You spilt paint for the living room on my wedding dress.

Jamie –

Lisa I had to get another one last minute.

Jamie It looked lovely. And the . . . (*He gestures.*)

Lisa Veil. It wasn't the one I wanted.

Jamie It looked fine.

Lisa 'Fine'!

Pause.

Anyway, I don't mind if you go or don't go.

Jamie Really?

She gestures a 'why not'.

I don't want to come off 'rude'.

Pause.

Lisa You can still make it if you leave right now.

Jamie I could fib and say I'm sick.

Lisa Like what?

Jamie Make something up.

Pause.

If I just don't go – don't go, don't turn up, it means . . . What does it mean?

Lisa If you don't go, it means question mark.

She goes.
    Jamie sits there. Eventually, he takes his tie off.
He calls out a little.

Jamie Does it mean question mark over me, or question mark over them?

She comes back in.

67

Jamie and Lisa's kitchen, the day of the fete.

Jamie comes home with a bunch of flowers. He puts them on the table. He looks a mess, like he's sweated and run around a lot.

Lisa comes in from the other room in leisure wear. Jamie starts unpacking his pannier. He takes out his water bottle, then a series of small packages wrapped in newspaper.

Lisa looks at the flowers.

Pause.

Lisa picks up the packages.

Lisa Didn't they sell in the end?

Jamie Half of them sold. I bought the rest of them back.

Lisa You brought them, or you bought them back?

Jamie *Bought.*

Lisa That was nice. Must have cost you a bit.

Pause.

What time did you do that?

Jamie Two-ish.

Pause.

Lisa So at two, you bought the remaining half of the gingerbread men back?

Jamie Yeah.

Lisa But the fair, the fete, went on from twelve to four p.m.

Jamie Yes.

Lisa So if, halfway through, half of them had sold, why did you take the rest off the table?

68

Jamie In case they didn't sell.

Lisa But they were selling, half of them had sold, halfway through the day.

Jamie We always have too much stuff left over.

Lisa That's OK, isn't it?

Jamie I didn't want your gingerbread men not to sell.

Lisa But they were selling out.

Jamie If at four o'clock, they were still there . . . I don't know. It would have been embarrassing.

Pause.

I didn't like to take the risk.

Pause.

And because . . . I organised the fete.

Lisa OK.

She reaches out for them.

Jamie Some of them are a bit . . . broken now.

Pause.

Whoops. It's like we're at RAF Lyneham! And these are the troops, coming back from Afghanistan . . . Sorry!

Lisa They were civilian gingerbread men.

He picks one up with arms missing. He's messing about.

Jamie Local militia then. This one's a double amputee . . . Oh dear, you have been in the wars.

He picks up an unidentifiable piece.

Body bag for you, sir!

He chucks it in the bin.

You know, nine times out of ten a soldier who gets shot, well, they got shot because they, what they call 'equivocated'. It's not as they expected and – the terrain or the heat, and they sort of panic or freeze, and then it goes wrong. Soldiers are trained to expect the unexpected.
I went with my instincts.

Lisa To buy back the gingerbread men?

Jamie Yes.

Lisa I think it was probably over-cautious.

Jamie I did what I thought was right at the time.

Lisa –

Jamie You know I wanted to join the SAS.

Lisa Yes, love.

Jamie Don't laugh!.

Lisa Isn't SAS when they jump out of planes and rescue hostages in the middle of the night?

Jamie I would have done it, if I hadn't felt so strongly about – teaching primary.

She glares at him.

Lisa The thing is. It was the joy of baking something and taking it to sell at the school fete. I got into it, I got excited and then you ruined the idea of it.

Pause.

Jamie I got you some flowers.
And some bread.

Lisa Thank you. Thanks, that's nice. Did Danny make this? The bread?

Jamie I don't know.

Lisa It looks like it has pumpkin seeds in it. Yum.

Jamie Does it?

Lisa Yes, and it looks, well, to me, it looks organic.

Jamie Does Danny bake?

Lisa You know he does. You know he makes the best bread ever. None of the mums round here sit at home making organic pumpkin-seed bread. Mind if I have a slice now?

Jamie I thought I'd have it for when you're away. If you slice it now, it won't keep as long.

Lisa Oh, OK. You keep it, special. I was a bit peckish, that's all.

Pause.

Seems like Danny has really settled in at the school.

Jamie He has. Everyone loves him.

Lisa You get on OK?

Jamie He's great.

Lisa He seems like the type who could end up running a school.

Jamie A primary school.

Lisa Well, yes, a primary school. I mean he's got vision.

Jamie –

Lisa Me and Joe went to his welcome assembly . . .

Jamie I wouldn't call Danny a visionary.

Lisa I didn't say 'visionary', I said he's got vision. As in, he looks ahead. He pictures things in a way that is really positive. And practical. He brings people on board, the way he sort of expresses himself. It's impressive.

Jamie I suppose so.

Lisa He gets the motor running on things. If he's involved, you want to be part of it, recycling whatever. A part of his energy.

Jamie Yes.

Lisa He's a real live wire to listen to. He's exciting, don't you think?

Jamie Yes.

Lisa Not like any kind of teacher I ever had or ever imagined having. He's brave and courageous and awake . . . to the world. That's the feeling I get.

Jamie Yes.

Lisa He really does have a kind of vision. Maybe I did mean it, maybe I did mean to say he's a visionary.

Pause.

Jamie He isn't perfect, you know?

Lisa No?

Jamie Oh no. Sometimes he can be late. Sometimes he is five, ten, fifteen minutes late for the start of school and this means . . . well, no teacher can afford to be late for school.

Lisa There are always teaching assistants aren't there, to help out or fill in?

Jamie Yes and no. And sometimes he meanders off-track and the teaching assistants talk about how inspiring and gifted he is, but I sometimes think it's their way of complaining too. Of flagging it up. To management.

Lisa That seems a complicated way of going about things.

Jamie Primary school teachers are complex.

Lisa I'm sure you told me about how he was late, once, because it turned out he had a doctor's appointment, and someone had just forgotten to cover, but it was written down. I remember because you were annoyed about the 'communication breakdown'.

Jamie Maybe.

Lisa So really he was late, once.

Pause.

Jamie Once, once or twice. And you know. Everybody at school knows he's married and that he's married to Joe. But I do feel like I have to defend him sometimes.

Lisa Do people say things about him?

Jamie No, not as such, but sometimes I feel the need to remind everyone that Danny deserves to be treated as an equal. To be treated just like everybody else. He's not unusual, he's not special.

Lisa Oh, but I think he is special. Did he buy any of my gingerbread men?

Jamie No.

Pause.

He did when I said you made them. Then he ate one and he made 'mmm, yum-yum' noises and said to say how much he liked them, then he bought a few more. Ten more.

Lisa So 'he didn't buy any'?

Jamie He did. He bought eleven in total. But he did it very quickly. And hardly said anything. Except to say what I just told you.

Pause.

It's more people worry what he does at the weekend. At school, he's great. But people are curious about his life after school and at the weekends. I'm not. I know him and Joe.

Lisa Are they still thinking of adopting? I didn't like to ask.

Jamie Not really.

Lisa When I last saw Danny he said they were.

Jamie They've applied. They're in the applications process. They've had their meetings. They're waiting for approval.

Lisa Are Danny and Joe still going to adopt, Jamie?

Jamie They want to, looks that way. Things are progressing.

Lisa How exciting for them.

Jamie Well. You can't have everything.

Lisa Jamie, I'm going to get ready to go to my mum's.

Jamie I'll put the flowers in water.

Lisa (*her mouth full*) I can do it.

Jamie We raised enough money for some new computers.

Lisa Did you?

Jamie We raised more than last year.

Lisa Oh, well done.

Jamie I feel quite proud. It was a success.

Lisa The kids'll be –

Jamie They deserve it. You know one of them called me 'gay' today.

Lisa Which one?

Jamie Richard.

Lisa Isn't he the –

Jamie He's a – tall.

Lisa Did he mean gay like the congestion charge is gay, or gay like Elton John?

Jamie Elton John.

Lisa Was it to do with your shoes?

Jamie What's wrong with deck shoes?

Lisa Where were his parents?

Jamie Raffle.

Pause.

Danny said I handled the situation exactly like you're meant to. Textbook.

Pause.

Lisa What is the textbook reply?

Jamie Oh . . . the truth.

Lisa Which is?

Pause.

Jamie It's OK to be gay . . .

Pause.

It's wrong to suggest someone is gay.
  It's OK to talk about it.
  Maybe, don't bring it up.

75

Lisa You said all that?

Jamie Very obliquely.

Lisa Well done for handling that.

Jamie smiles.

If Joe and Danny adopt, can they get a mixed-race child?

Jamie I don't know. Why?

Lisa Nothing.

Pause.

Trendy.

Jamie If they get, say, a five-year-old. Straight into school, double income, no childcare costs, no sleep deprivation. That's clever.

Jamie eats a gingerbread man and chews it.

I'll put the flowers in some water, baby.

Lisa Oh, don't call me that. I can't stand it.

Jamie Sorry.

Lisa You always take half of them out.

Jamie The point is, I've handled everything pretty well.

Lisa –

Jamie Yeah. I'm sorry, about the gingerbread men. I didn't understand. About the joy of it.

Lisa You always tell me how imaginative you are.

Jamie *Creative.* I'm a *creative* person.

He fills a vase with water. Puts the flowers in.

At work. I can sometimes hear Danny teaching in the room next door.

He extracts a few. Then a few more.

Lisa OK.

Jamie It makes me freeze up. It's like I suddenly have absolutely no idea what I'm doing. And then I panic.

Jamie looks at the vase, then at Lisa.

THREE

It's late. Jamie is surrounded by exercise books. He has gold-star stickers stuck to his sleeve. He marks the books, occasionally, applying a gold star from his sleeve to the page.

The house phone rings. He doesn't answer.

Jamie looks out of the window, goes and checks the door is locked, pulling another bolt across. He turns a main light off and puts on a side light.

He takes several pieces of paper out of a drawer. He looks at them and turns them over, lining them up. He takes a red pen out of the drawer and corrects the spelling from 'fagot' to 'faggot'. He reviews his work, bins it and corrects another one.

Jamie makes a call.

Jamie Hi Lisa – yep call me back when you're not busy.
Lisa?
Quick, quick thing.
Do you happen to know where my Julie London record is? No? OK. No reason. It helps me to relax, that's all.
I don't know.
No problem.
Speak in a bit.

He hangs up.
He sings quietly.

Now you say you're sorry
For being so untrue . . .

*He bundles up those flyers and the rest from the
drawer and binds them neatly using an elastic band.
Jamie picks up the phone again. Dials. Waits.*

It's me. How's things? You all right? Yeah? Do you think
you could come round? I'm all right. I'm OK. Lisa's away.
We could watch the match or something. OK. Thank
you. See you in a bit . . . Or, if it's tricky, then tomorrow
just as easily. Tomorrow is just as good. Thanks, Dad.
Actually you know what, I meant come over tonight will
you, yeah, yeah. OK, OK. Love you.

Silence.
Jamie checks the door again.
The phone rings.

Jamie Hello?
  What?
  Lisa? Oh hello, Mrs . . . Mrs Walters?
  Oh. Yes. Right. Of course I remember you. That is
right, yes. And your son, your daughter, that's right.
Jennifer. OK, yes. How is she?
  Is she? That is excellent.
  I mean, everyone is, that's what we. Learning
difficulties are normal nowadays. In the sense that they
come up. Now and again. It's my job really to, try and
help. To spot it if I see it.
  No. I mean . . . She's won a prize? Huh.
  That's – No, Mrs Walters. I'm really pleased. I'm really
pleased that everything is turning out so well for Jennifer.
Good for Jennifer. Good for her.
  She's a great kid. She has lovely red hair doesn't she,
and a cracking smile. That's it.
  Well . . . good. And how are you?
  That's good to hear.

78

I'm still at Willows, that's right. (*He jokes.*) Eek.
Oh I don't know about that!
You. Are. Welcome!
Hardly!

He laughs politely.

Mrs Walters, I have to tell you that I am right in the middle of catching up on marking some drawings the class have done for the Tudors . . . Yes, it is advanced, you could say that. We like to push the boundaries at Willows, that we do.

Well . . . I had a day off yesterday. So that was nice. I don't know why I'm telling you this!

Well. I stayed at some friends and then took the day off and . . .

And it looks like it's very dark outside now.

Good.

OK now. Thank you so much for calling. Oh! A letter of recommendation? Of course I can do that for you. No problem at all, I am putty in your hands. You tell me what you need me to say for her to qualify for the Steel Drums classes (*He makes a note.*) Uh-huh, uh-huh. To-the-rescue. More than happy to help! Please do give my best to little, not-so-little-now Jennifer. Anything else, please do call the school.

All the best, b'bye. B'bye. Bye.

Jamie hangs up, pleased. He taps the table, satisfied.
Looks around, expectantly.
　　He sings. This time, for 'fun'.

Now you say you're sorry
For being so untrue . . .
Well you can cry me a river, cry me a river
I cried cried cried a river over you.

FOUR

Lisa is waiting at the table. Jamie comes in covered with blood.

Lisa I'm actually getting quite dizzy watching you dancing around.

Jamie I need to go for a run.

Jamie jumps on the spot.

Lisa Don't. Did Joe go back to make sure Danny's OK?

He nods.

Jamie Sorry about all this.

Lisa Yeah.

Jamie looks at his watch.

Jamie The police'll be here any minute. Are you OK?

Lisa Yes.

Jamie You sure?

Lisa Yes.

Jamie Do you want me to get you a paracetamol?

Lisa OK.

Jamie goes and comes back with a tablet. He puts it on the table.

And a jumper.

He goes and comes back with one.

Jamie Thank you.

Lisa Will you clean up any bits of blood that have gone on the floor?

80

Jamie Yes.

Lisa Do you promise?

Jamie Yes. The police will be here soon, then you can go back to your mum's and . . . watch a box set.

Lisa I'm not supposed to be stressing or it mucks up the IVF.

Jamie I know.

Lisa Because we agreed.

Jamie It's me who has to deal with the reality of his situation. I'm taking responsibility for Danny, for all of this.

Lisa This is *your* situation.

Jamie – Sure.

Lisa It's you in pain, isn't it?

Jamie I took an antihistamine.

Lisa I meant, inside or whatever. Like you're suffering?

Jamie Do you think I'm suffering?

Lisa Aren't you?

Jamie I can't ever tell.

Lisa It's your situation.

Jamie I don't see it like that.

Lisa Jamie.

Pause.

It's really not the right time to talk and you need to talk to the police. We've got egg retrieval in the morning, Mum's driving me there. And your face is . . .

Jamie I like it, leave it.

Lisa You're upset.

Jamie Am I?

Lisa I've never seen you like this.

Jamie What?

Lisa This.

Jamie What?

Lisa Pumped.

Jamie Really?

Jamie looks flattered.

You can tell me.

Lisa We can leave it.

Jamie No.

Lisa All right.

Jamie Just leave it then, or don't.

Lisa I think you're really quite – worried.

Jamie You can talk to me, Lisa.

Lisa I feel like you're getting more and more worried.

Pause.

Jamie OK.

Lisa I don't really like living with a – worried person, a worrier. It's the worst possible state to live – constant worry.

Pause.

Jamie What did you want to talk about?

Lisa It's hard to live with you sometimes . . .

Jamie It's hard to live with you sometimes.

Lisa OK.

Jamie OK.

Lisa OK to what?

Jamie OK.

Lisa Jamie, what's OK?

Jamie Nothing. It's OK.

Lisa There are some things I think about.

Jamie OK.

Lisa Yes, and some stuff I only started to notice recently.

Jamie Do you mean this?

He points to a very faint moustache.

I'm growing it.

Lisa Oh.

She inspects.

No.

Pause.

Jamie Yes?!

Lisa Your . . . (*bad luck*).

Jamie I can't do anything about my bad luck.

Lisa The school door that broke, that was a big thing at the time. I can't remember – your bike going in the canal, losing all the test results, your dad getting sick, lots of things.

Jamie Go on.

Lisa What?

Jamie Say it.

Lisa I'm not saying me not getting pregnant is your fault or anything to do with anything. No way, that's not what I'm saying. I just feel like you are a bit of a magnet for bad things at the moment. That you maybe in a way, create that. Or you want it.

Jamie If we're being superstitious. Isn't it women, traditionally, who bring bad luck? Like sailors wouldn't let women on board the boat. Maybe you're bad luck.

Silence.

Lisa Well. Is it anything to do with us, then – (*mouthing the words*) doing anal?

Pause.

Jamie No.

Pause.

I don't even like –

Lisa *I* don't (*mouthing the words*) like anal sex.

Jamie No, *I* told *you*, it – chafes.

Lisa You (*mouthing*) liked anal. Quite – a lot.

Jamie We've done it *twice*.

He resumes.

It's because *you're* worrying. You worry too much. You're worrying you won't get pregnant.

Lisa I won't if we keep doing it your way.

Jamie Twice!

Pause.

Lisa Maybe anal is bad luck. Which is why people are so funny about it?

Pause.

Jamie I don't feel like you, Lisa. I feel lucky. I don't worry about things the way you do. You really let small things, you let them feel much bigger, much more significant than they are. This – (*points to his face*) is significant. Am I allowed to be worried about this?

Lisa You can be worried about this.

Jamie I'm not though. I like it.

Silence.

Lisa Give me your phone then, to take a picture?

Jamie Yes please.

Lisa It's got better . . . thingy.

Jamie Resolution.

He hands her his phone. He sort of half poses. She takes a couple of pictures. He looks at them.

This is what someone who has been persecuted looks like.

Lisa You're not being persecuted.

Jamie Is this what you meant . . . ?

Lisa I doubt it.

Jamie . . . A sort of cosmic mix-up. I get Danny's bad stuff instead of him.

Lisa No.

Jamie Who Danny is, *leads –*

He draws a series of points in the air, joining up the dots . . .

– through the cosmic distortion filter, to me being attacked.

Lisa I meant a shift.

Jamie ?

Lisa A change. That's what I have been feeling.

Jamie OK.

Lisa For everyone.

Jamie ?

Lisa Something.

Jamie OK.

Lisa Something.

Jamie Like what?

Lisa Like . . . it's –

Jamie Yes . . .?

Lisa I'd prefer not to say.

Jamie Fine.

Lisa Nothing's going to change.

Jamie Because I don't think things need to change.

Lisa I know you don't.

Jamie Give over, Lisa!

Lisa I think you're involved in some sort of epic panic, Jamie. I think it started very small, when you found out Danny would be working at Willows, and it hasn't gone away. It's just got bigger and bigger and . . .

Jamie Sure.

Lisa It's like watching someone have a panic attack in slow motion over months. And you're so big it affects everyone else. Like a giant tree falling in a really lovely residential area . . .

Jamie (*interrupting*) Maybe the change is that – Maybe the change is that – Maybe the change . . .

Pause.

Maybe the change is that nothing at all has to change.

Lisa But you want it to change.

Jamie I want it to be how it was.

Lisa That's – change back.

Jamie sings nervously – 'Cry me a river . . . cry me a river . . .!'
Doorbell.
Jamie looks at the door.

Jamie It's the police.

Lisa I need to calm down before you talk to them.

Jamie OK.

He smiles.
Doorbell again.

Lisa We should be worrying about Danny.

Jamie People in the Renaissance, Lisa, they had the Enlightenment . . .

Pause.

We have getting the shit kicked out of you by people you don't know, on the street in the middle of the day. It's the most life-affirming thing that's ever happened to me. I knew things were going to get worse for me, broadly speaking, and they have! Do you have any idea how consoling that is?

Jamie skips up and answers the door.
Joe and Jamie come in together.

Lisa Joe? (*To Jamie.*) You told me he got out and went back for Danny.

Jamie leans on Joe.

Joe I was just driving around outside to try and get my head straight.

Lisa Jamie!

Joe I'm sorry to put you through all this, Lisa. He's all right isn't he, our Jamie? He's all right.

Jamie Oh stop . . .!

No one laughs at Jamie pretending to be camp.

It's lovely to have you here.

Joe Thanks. It's a lovely old kitchen.

Jamie It's just a rental or we'd do it up . . . hopefully my dad's going to help us out with a deposit . . . though we'd never live in a new-build. Nothing after the 1930s.

He looks to Lisa, expecting confirmation.

Lisa I don't understand what Danny's done wrong.

Joe He wouldn't leave the house, that's all.

Lisa But he's going to get hurt, isn't he?

Jamie He won't 'deviate course', will he? Let Joe relax half a minute.

Joe Danny's waiting for a 'phone call'. He's convinced.

Lisa I'm worried about Danny.

Pause.

Joe I've never even seen Danny cry.

Lisa He's all on his own. Did you call him?

Joe He won't answer! No chance!

Jamie Not like me, I'm always having a cry, Joe.

Lisa stares at them, then as no one else moves she grabs her coat. Jamie blocks her leaving. He holds her.

Worry about *me*.

FIVE

Lisa is dressed for work. She vomits in the sink, it trails on the floor as she stands upright.
Jamie comes in, half awake, like he hasn't slept anyway.

Jamie What time does it finish then?

Lisa Nine-to-five-ish, isn't it.

Jamie She ill, is she?

Lisa It's him, it's my old colleague. He's on sick leave.

Jamie They've got you in?

Lisa Just for a bit.

Jamie Good luck then. Have a nice day.

Pause.

Make sure you come back! (*He smiles like he's joking.*) I haven't slept a wink.

Lisa You do look tired. But it's just for a bit, isn't it? We need the . . .

Jamie That's right.

Pause.

You've got no idea what it's like –

Pause.

– to sit outside the head teacher's office, like you're six. Waiting to be approved of. Waiting to be told, you're all right, you're good enough.

And then they look at you funny.

Lisa You said. I can't get there late . . .

Jamie And they go through who you are and what you're about and stuff you've done, and what they're worried you might do. And they say tombola, and nativity, and Reading Corner like it was a bad thing to do. And they chat about it all. They 'confer' in their 'conflab'. And they take a view on it. What's best for the kids. What's best for everyone. Maybe I need a bit of time 'for me' to think things through. 'Am *I* happy?'

Lisa Are you?

Jamie I don't think they know what they're doing. They're so forwards they're backwards. No one even felt sorry I'd been beaten up. It was like they thought it was about time. It was time. That I deserved it. Someone like me deserved it. Because I've had it so easy. I don't think it has been easy. No one's even come round.

I don't want to be one any more. I can't do it.

Lisa A teacher?

Jamie Be a man, Lisa. I don't want to be a man any more. It's so humiliating.

They got me apologising to Richard. I told him I was sorry for making him cry. I had to bend my knees over so I was level with him.

Lisa puts her bag down.

He said that he'd done a new activity with Mrs Collins. He said everyone had been given a piece of paper. They all scrunched up the bits of paper, stamped on them with their shoes on, and then gave them back to Mrs Collins.

They were all told to hold it to her face and say 'sorry'. Then Mrs Collins said, 'But sorry isn't enough, is it? You have to think about other people's feelings first. Because you can't ever fix that piece of paper to make it how it was again. Never ever.'

And then I must have looked, I don't know, hurt, because he gave me some advice. He said, 'Be true to yourself.'

Lisa Oh . . .

Jamie I gave him a thumbs-up to show I understood. (*He does thumbs-up.*) Be true to yourself.

I felt *this* big.

He nods, emotional.

I don't want to be one any more.

I can't.

Lisa looks at him, unsure if she should go or stay with him.

Lisa Everything feels a bit –

He takes her hand.

Nicer.

She touches his face, looks at him in wonder.

SIX

Danny's standing in Lisa's kitchen. His waterproof is wet, dripping on a hook. The place is a mess.

Danny I was supposed to come round when Jamie was here. I told Joe I'd do that.

Lisa Really?

She lingers awkwardly.

Danny I promised Joe I'd make the gesture. He wanted it to be face-to-face.

Pause.

Lisa Sorry about the mess.

Danny Joe says, I've put Jamie in a bit of a bad position at school.

She tries to clear a space in the mess.

I feel bad.

She interrupts.

Lisa Honestly, he's much better. He thinks the world is right back on his side. You'd not believe the difference. Just this – (*Points to her stomach.*) He thinks he's won.

Danny Won what?

Lisa Just, won.

She looks at him blankly.

You know, I think I managed to get pregnant by literally doing nothing. I just do nothing. Keep doing nothing, feet up, relax, relax, don't worry about everything, and everything will be OK. Everything ends up OK. You can't force it. That's what Jamie said all along – we shouldn't have to *do* anything. 'Just be us.'

Pause.

But I want to say congratulations.

Danny No! Congratulations to you!

Lisa No! I wanted to say it to you!

Danny Oh thanks, thanks! But congratulations to you!

Lisa I feel like you can say that so much better than I can. I really mean it, I mean congratulations to you.

Danny I know. Thank you! It's fucking ace. Congratulations!

Lisa Jamie couldn't believe it. He felt blessed. You know, like things had turned a corner.

Danny I feel that!

Lisa Jamie felt renewed.

Danny We'll get confirmation on which kid very soon. But we're in, we're approved of.

Pause.

I'm getting the room ready.

Lisa Me too!

Danny Of course you are. Fuckin' ace.

Pause.

Lisa Jamie said – they told him they wanted to use your boat game as a model for the whole school. I think it's amazing. You're so clever.

Danny Yeah.

Lisa You're so clever. You must be happy.

Danny I'm chuffed to bits. All those little people going into the world more confident. I'm chuffed at the idea of it.

Lisa Shall I just tell him you came round?

Pause.

Danny I've got five minutes if he's on his way.

Pause.

I've asked for it to be a one-off for now, so I can have a little think.

Lisa Oh no.

Danny Yeah.

Lisa Danny, you have to, don't you?

Danny shrugs.

It's inspiring, isn't it? Don't worry about Jamie. He'll get another job.

Pause.

Easily. *You* can't back down.

Danny Well . . .

Lisa Is it because of those lads?

Danny I've got Joe to think about . . .

Lisa Oh.

Danny We've decided, for the adoption, to keep everything else –

Lisa Oh.

Danny He wants me to let him take the lead for a while, make decisions. He thinks I've, he said I've put us at risk.

Pause.

I feel tired, to be honest.

Lisa Really?

Danny Yeah.

Lisa I'd be worried about the kids missing out, I think.

Danny Nah.

Lisa Seriously.

Danny Nah . . .

Lisa And what about your own kid?

Danny We'll see.

Lisa It's weird. I don't feel tired at all.

Pause.

Danny So Joe and I wanted to officially invite you and Jamie round for dinner to celebrate. Joe says you and Jamie of all people will understand how important it is to celebrate getting pregnant or nearly, nearly getting a kid to adopt.

Lisa That sounds lovely, really lovely, that sounds really nice.

Danny It matters to Joe, that we all see eye to eye. Joe wants things to be what-do-you-call-it – calmer.

Lisa I can understand that.

Danny All calm down.

Lisa All calm.

Danny Yes.

Lisa Calm before the storm.

Danny Anyway, I'm here to invite you both to dinner.

Pause.

Lisa Danny, I really was looking forward to saying, 'This is your teacher Mr Thompson,' to our kid. And the day you do your special class. I was going to get us to move house if we needed to make sure that would happen. I'll have to look forward to something else now.

Danny Thanks for that. Means a lot.

Lisa Such a shame.

Danny Yeah.

Silence.

Lisa Did you always know you were gay?

Danny I think so. Four, I was four.

Suddenly emotional.

It's the kitchen table. Saying this stuff out loud at the kitchen table . . . Sorry! Classic. I don't know what's wrong with me. I feel a bit, over-exposed.

Lisa But you're so good, Danny, you always have the words for everything.

Danny Growing up, I always felt a bit like a black kid in a white family who don't really know they don't like black people. It was fine, but.

Lisa Oh, I think being black would be much worse, Danny.

Pause.

I'd like to do your boat class, I think. Get all that understanding. Be able to get people to understand.

Danny Joe suggested Sunday.

Lisa Will you do a roast?

Danny Can do.

Lisa We usually have a roast on Sunday. Jamie can't live without it.

Danny We can do a roast.

Lisa Not if you don't usually. What do you normally eat on a Sunday?

Danny I don't know. I was thinking paella?

Lisa Paella?

Pause.

Don't invite us.

Danny I'm inviting you.

Lisa Why don't you come to us, then? I'll cook.

Danny I told Joe I'd invite you to ours.

Lisa It might just be easier. And then you don't have to cook.

Danny I like cooking.

Lisa Actually I don't know if I'm up to having people round. It's a big thing, cooking for double.

Danny OK.

Lisa I shouldn't have suggested dinner. Maybe we can think again in a few weeks.

Danny I'll tell Joe you can't come?

Lisa No, I'm just saying I shouldn't have suggested it because it's a bad time for me to have lots of people round.

Danny OK. Thanks for the invitation.

Lisa You're really so welcome. We love having you. We'll do it another time.

Pause.

Talk to Joe.

Danny I will.

Lisa Convince him.

Danny Definitely.

Lisa *You're* not allowed to give up.

Danny Yeah.

Lisa You won't be the kind of parent you want to be.

Danny Maybe.

Lisa You've got the gift of explaining things.

Danny Thanks.

Lisa Some people can't learn.

Danny Yeah.

Lisa Ignore them. Ignore us. People like us.

Danny Yeah.

Lisa Pretend we're not here.

Danny Yeah.

Lisa You're our hero.

Pause.

Anyway. Congratulations.

Pause.

Are you getting a mixed-race one?

Danny No.

Lisa No.

They both look to the window.

Danny If Jamie was here I'd like to make things right with him.

Jamie comes home. He's a wearing a tracksuit, he hasn't been at work. He's confident, relaxed.
He sees Danny, gives Lisa a kiss. Danny watches Lisa, uncomfortable.

Jamie Hi, baby.

Lisa Hi, baby.

She stands up, he sits down, opposite Danny, his legs outstretched.

Danny Hi, Jamie. How are you?

Pause.

I'm sorry about the job, Jamie.

Jamie shrugs, puts his arms out wide like he doesn't care.

Jamie She tell you she's pregnant?

Jamie whistles cheerfully, gets up, looks through the cupboards until he finds a snack bar, which he unwraps and eats.

Danny Congratulations.

Pause.

Joe, *we*, want you to come round or something, at some point. That's why I'm here, to invite you. You used to come over all the time.

Jamie I can't eat anything at the moment, mate. I'm missing a couple of teeth. I don't mean to probe, but are you here out of gay curiosity or is there something . . . ?

Danny walks around a bit, unsure what to do.

Danny Look, by the time those lads you ran into came round to mine, they'd run out of steam and . . .

Jamie And you have a way of talking to people. I know! I've seen you at it. You're doing it now. Voodoo Danny!

He picks up a colander and puts it in front of his face.

Danny I'm sorry I didn't believe why they were after you.

Jamie I was gay-bashed?

Danny Yes.

Jamie Old school.

Danny Isn't it? You don't think it happens any more.

Jamie All the time, all the time. I've googled it.

Pause.

But they didn't bash *you*?

Danny I was on the phone.

Jamie You all had a cup of Earl Grey tea.

Danny That's . . .

Jamie What?

Danny We had a chat . . .

Jamie You didn't call the police?

Danny They were coming round to yours.

Jamie No one's been arrested.

Danny I'm sorry.

Lisa Jamie.

Jamie There was me worrying it was just for being a twat. Like you said.

Danny Like I said, we want to make you a paella sometime. Come over and have some food with us. Midweek maybe if Sunday's no good.

Jamie Paella?

Danny Or . . .

Jamie (*exasperated*) No one wants to eat paella, Danny! Chorizo, chicken *and* prawn?! Together?!

He puts up the colander.

Danny I didn't want you to get hurt or lose your job just for being a bit . . . unaware. Joe says . . .

Jamie It's suddenly very easy to get rid of teachers no one likes very much, isn't it? What sort of prejudice do you call that in your class?

Danny Joe says, I get excited. That I overreach. That maybe I've pushed you.

Jamie lowers the colander.

It's sort of hard to explain, isn't it . . . where I'm coming from? . . . It's something to do with – You have a beautiful singing voice, don't you?

Pause.

I think maybe you should sing more. Your voice is fucking lovely. I reckon it would feel good, to stop holding on, so – tight. Wouldn't it feel good, to be someone who sings really fucking loudly? And it's beautiful and you don't care.

Jamie I don't want to *sing*.

Danny Or . . . Sorry.

Pause.

I'm sorry.

Lisa Don't say sorry.

Jamie puts the colander down.

Jamie It's like *you're* a bit of a bully, in a way, deputy.

Danny I'm not deputy head until next term.

Jamie You could put in a word.

Danny Jamie, Willows aren't going to . . .

Jamie No probs then!

Danny They want to do training with all the staff. They've gone full-on liberal to the fucking max, even I'm a bit shy of it at the moment. The admin and cleaners, the whole lot. So people get comfortable with particular words in their mouths. There are things people find hard to say.

Jamie The cleaners? They say anything.

Danny There's some stuff, people don't know how to say out loud. They don't know how to make it feel normal.
   They think those words do something to them, like they're bad luck.

Jamie He's off again.

   Jamie thinks.

Lisa Danny, Jamie loves Willows.

Danny I know!

Lisa There's a chalk outline of his hand on one of the playground floor tiles. His name is on a brick at the back. Heart and soul – and they know it.

Jamie They'd give me my job back tomorrow if they feel I've 'rebranded', made an effort. Jamie hashtag Jamie 2.0.

Danny Maybe.

Jamie I could say getting beaten up made me realise . . .

Danny OK . . .

Jamie Some stuff.

Lisa Like he's been a bit . . .

Jamie Emotional. I was *gay-bashed*.

Lisa If he can present it right, like he's part of their future plans, that there's a reason, he's been through something, he's *evolved* . . . with you on board, don't you think?

Pause.

Danny Lisa?

Pause.

Maybe, yeah.

Jamie And would you support me to the school?

Pause.

Joe seemed to think you might.

Danny I can try.

Jamie V. good.

Danny If I can.

Jamie You've just got all the words, don't you? All the words that make you sound – good?

Danny It's about admitting you have prejudices or something. Being willing to change. It's not fully fleshed out.

Jamie That's it! Stuff like that! If you're up for it . . . ?

Danny If you . . . yeah, then OK.

Jamie Then you're a mate, Danny.

Danny Yeah.

Jamie How's Joe?

Danny He's – lovely.

Jamie You got a kid yet?

Danny Nearly. She's two.

Jamie A girl?!

Pause.

Lisa Have a seat, Danny.

Jamie Lisa . . . kettle.

She flicks the switch. Danny thinks about sitting down, then doesn't.

All right . . . ?

Danny Just so I've got this straight in my own head . . . before we start . . .

Jamie Yes, mate, go on.

Danny When Richard . . .

Jamie Richard?

Danny Richard in Year Two, Zebra class.

Jamie OK.

Danny Called you gay to . . . the other little lad . . .

Jamie Adam.

Danny Adam! You got wound up, didn't you?

Jamie – You know, I can't remember.

Danny OK. Fair enough.

Pause.

It's not a trick. I just wanted to know. It seemed like you were –

Jamie OK. But I don't think so. I'd remember that.

Danny I remember how worried you were when you came round after the fete.

Jamie I don't remember. Sorry.

Danny It really got to you.

Jamie I overreacted.

Danny You were embarrassed.

Jamie I don't think I was.

Danny It *got* under your skin.

Jamie Richard's a cock, remember.

Danny But you were the grown-up. And you had an opportunity.

Jamie This was ages ago. Yes. To do what?

Danny To make it OK.

Jamie You said I did what I thought was best and that's OK. You patted my leg, remember?

Pause.

Danny Yes. Just so I can help you. Not help you, give you some pointers, before we start, so I know where we are – Could you say, let's say, 'lesbian'.

Jamie Is this one of those activities where the activity never takes place? The activity *is* talking about the activity?

Danny 'Lesbian'. Or OK just, I don't know – 'queer'.

Jamie Yes, mate.

Pause.

Just teach me stuff to say to Willows. I've got a kid on the way, mate!

Danny What do you think 'gay' means?

Jamie What?

Danny What do you think 'gay' means?

Jamie You tell me!

Danny Say 'I'm gay'.

Jamie After all this?

Danny For pretend.

Jamie OK.

Danny For a laugh?!

Jamie For a laugh!

Danny To feel the words in your mouth.

Jamie Yeah.

Danny To get them to come out normal.

Jamie Feels weird.

Danny It's OK. This is silly. Say: 'I slept with another man. I love him.' Out loud.

Jamie –

Danny Why not, Jamie?

Jamie It's silly.

Danny For pretend?

Jamie What's the 'learning objective'?!

Danny What's the learning objective . . .

Pause.

It shouldn't feel funny. Saying 'I'm gay' shouldn't feel funny. It should feel normal. No one's going to overhear and word won't get around, and it's not bad luck. Say 'I'm gay'. For fun. 'I'm gay'.

Danny gets up, frustrated.

Jamie I'm gay.

Jamie takes a glass of water. He sips it, swilling subtly as he swallows.

(*To Lisa.*) I'm not gay.

Lisa I know.

Jamie (*to Danny*) Come on then.

Danny looks at his watch.

Danny This is Year One stuff. This is basic, isn't it?

He gathers up his things, surprised at himself for starting to lose it.

Jamie You're not being very inclusive again, Danny.

Danny You and Joe, you both got brought up thinking it was bad.

Jamie Joe's gay.

Danny Doesn't stop him thinking it's not normal.

Danny looks at Jamie, weary.

Jamie When Joe was still married to Kate, I was one of the first people he told he was – in love with a man. Has he told you this? Someone should have told you this. (*To Lisa.*) Did you tell him this yet? (*Continuing.*) I held his soggy heart in my hands for *five* hours. When someone tells you that . . . they are gay.

Pause.

I felt, in charge. I was in charge of that 'experience'. I took him to Pizza Express. He had a starter and beer, pizza each, we shared a pud. I paid. I didn't have a starter or a drink. I made it easy for him.

Danny You're not in charge . . .

Lisa looks at Danny, then Jamie, then back at Danny.

Jamie Willows is special you know. You're lucky. But after a few years you might want to move somewhere else, and then they'll know, you're the teacher who did the gay lesson and you have this agenda.

Danny I want Willows to be a nice place for everyone.

Jamie And you'll have to go there and be the gay teacher. You'll be 'gay Danny'. And you'll wish you hadn't said anything.

Silence.

There's a school up the road next the church. I used to do temp work for them. Faith school. They do very good wall displays. My dad has a friend who used to teach there. Their nativity plays are a bit orthodox. But . . . It's good. It's a v. normal school. It's important everyone can be true to themselves. Isn't it?

Jamie gets up, lingers a moment. Goes.
 Danny gets his coat.

Lisa Don't go yet.

Danny You'll be fine, promise.

Lisa What am I supposed to do?

Danny I don't know.

Lisa You do know. Be braver or what or . . .?

Danny You're like little kids waving your arms around, shouting out, pretending to be drowning at sea.

Lisa –

Danny I can't *save* you . . .

Silence.

She's called Cara. The little girl we want to be our daughter. Cara.

He crosses his fingers.

Lisa I meant to ask.

Lisa looks at him expectantly.

Feels like I'm sinking.

Danny Does it?

Lisa Yeah.

Pause.

Danny I don't know what to tell you . . . Pretend to swim. Swim.

Danny zips his waterproof right up. He looks out.